DEMOCRACY ON TRIAL

DEMOCRACY ON TRIAL

JEAN BETHKE ELSHTAIN

BasicBooks
A Division of HarperCollins*Publishers*

Copyright © 1995 by Jean Bethke Elshtain.
Published by BasicBooks,
A Division of HarperCollins Publishers, Inc.

Designed by Ellen Levine

LIBRARY OF CONGRESS CATALOGING-IN-PUBLICATION DATA
Elshtain, Jean Bethke, 1941–
    Democracy on trial / Jean Bethke Elshtain.
        p.   cm.
    Includes bibliographical references and index.
    ISBN 0–465–01616–2 (cloth)
    ISBN 0–465–01617–0 (paper)
    1. Democracy—United States. 2. United States—Politics
and government.   I. Title.
JK31.E57 1995
324.6'3'0973—dc20   94–31665
                                                            CIP

96 97 98 99 ❖/HC 9 8 7 6 5 4 3 2 1

To the memory of my father,
PAUL G. BETHKE,
a man of democratic temperament.
1912–1993

CONTENTS

ACKNOWLEDGMENTS

This book first saw the light of day as part of the 1993 Massey Lectures I was invited and honored to give in the fall of that year. Special thanks to Bernie Lucht, Executive Producer of Ideas; Jill Eisen, for keeping me on track; and Jamie Swift, who first had the idea. Jill Saddlemeyer, master of Massey College, was a gracious hostess.

PREFACE

"DISAGREEMENT," noted the great American Catholic pluralist John Courtney Murray, "is not an easy thing to reach." The aim of this book is to reach disagreement. Arriving at that principled yet pragmatic point seems harder all the time. We citizens of the United States are told by the young and the angry and the old, who should know better, that it is no longer possible for us to speak to one another; that we, quite literally, inhabit our own little islands of bristling difference where we comport with those just like ourselves: no outsiders are welcome. This is an astonishing idea for an American to express and all the more astonishing for its frequency. One recent example that made headlines was the explanation offered by a group of black students from a California high school for giggling at a showing of Steven Spielberg's *Schindler's List*. Commenting on their reaction to that film and to other efforts to "teach them" about the Holocaust, one sixteen-year-old girl told a reporter, "We should have been in classrooms learning about the real deal." And that "real deal" concerns "our own culture before someone else's." Translated into the separatist politics of the present, this statement means that we should learn about *our* culture and *nobody else's*. These ardent young people were giving voice to a legitimate concern, but in language that will only deepen their sense of isolation and despair over time.

Of course, one must understand that the student quoted by the press is young and angry and that youth and racial injustice are sufficient reasons to account for sassiness. But it is the particular *form* this "repudiation" takes—I do not know what else to call it. It is not political rebellion, but what Nietzsche might have considered the pernicious corrosion of resentment, that prods concern and foreboding. The language of opposition now appears as a cascading series of manifestos that tell us we cannot live together; we cannot work together; we are not in this together; we are not Americans who have something in common, but racial, ethnic, gender, or sexually identified clans who demand to be "recognized" only or exclusively as "different." Think about how odd this is on the face of it: I require that *you* recognize that *we* have nothing in common with one another. This demand is rapidly becoming a shared civic zaniness that threatens to implode our culture. We are in danger of losing democratic civil society. It is that simple and that dangerous, springing, as it does, not from a generous openness to sharp disagreement—democratic feistiness—but from a cynical and resentful closing off of others. We are all involved in the process—those of us who fight it, those of us who celebrate it, and those of us who acquiesce in it. No one escapes. The long history of the human race suggests that resentment breeds resentment; hatred fuels hatred; isolation feeds paranoia; cynicism stokes mistrust; and fear generates flight from neighborliness, largeheartedness, and the patience necessary to perdure.

When I told a distinguished scholar that I was going to call this book of reflections on our perils and our present but fading possibilities *Democracy on Trial*, he commented that the title had a "very 1940s ring to it." His response gave me pause, but only for a moment. Upon reflection, I decided I liked the analogy. To be sure, American democracy today is not confronted by "the dictators," haters and destroyers of democracy abroad, but by the repudiation of democracy in its most generous incarnations from within. During the earlier crisis that haunted Western democracies, Reinhold Niebuhr wrote two of his great works, *The Nature and Destiny of Man* and *The Children of Light and the Children of Darkness*. He challenged those who insisted that democracy must be based on sunny propositions about the innate goodness of human beings. Theses about our goodness invite Manichaean constructions about our condition. If something "bad" is going on, it is those nasty guys out there who are doing evil things to us. But the truth is that evil lurks within. Each of us carries in us the capacity for both goodness and hatred, for both creating community and sowing the seeds of petty strife.

Niebuhr argued that democratic institutions are, at one and the same time, the "cause" and the "consequence, of cultural variety and social pluralism."[1] They are, for that very reason, uniquely vulnerable to a variety of hammer blows from friends and enemies alike. If we spurn those institutional forms and matrices that enable us to negotiate our differences and to mediate them in civil and political ways, the result will be not more variety and pluralism but less. If we continue to move toward the creation of "separate" institutions and pedagogies and "cultures," we will invite not more variety and pluralism but less. Martin Luther King, Jr., understood that idea when he moved to "out-Jefferson Jefferson," in the words of the scholar Cornel West. He called us to, not away from, democratic citizenship. That does not mean a bland erosion of *distinctiveness*. But honoring our distinctions, as peoples of a particular heritage and individuals of particular gifts, is far different from the current construction of "difference" as a form of group homogeneity that brooks no disagreement or distinction *within* and can maintain itself only as a redoubt *against* threatening "enemies" from without, whether this takes the form of a walled-in garden suburb, academic balkanization (a word that, alas, has grown ever more apt), or political rallies to which no members of spurned groups or genders are admitted and during which they are demonized.

Just a year before the remarkable events of 1989 that turned the world upside down, the Polish playwright and novelist Janusz Glowacki reviewed a new production of Shakespeare's *Hamlet* in the *New York Times*. He had watched it with an audience of students at the Brooklyn Academy of Music and remarked that the entry of Fortinbras's army had been received with "carefree laughter" from the audience. Why? Because America "has not had any experience of loss of independence, foreign armies, or occupations." Glowacki, who has had such experience, did not laugh. "Not me," he wrote. "I belong to the nervous generation."[2] As an American who has passed her own mid-century mark, I have never known the loss of independence, foreign armies, or occupations, but I have joined the ranks of the nervous generation. I believe we are in the danger zone. No outside power will take us over

and destroy our freedom. We are perfectly capable, my ner-
vousness tells me, of doing that to ourselves, all in the name of
more freedom. Jean-Jacques Rousseau lamented the way civi-
lized man, in his exalted self-love, rushed to embrace his
chains, thinking he was clasping freedom to his bosom. Why
should we lucky people, we Americans, be immune? The pro-
tagonist of Wallace Stegner's wonderful novel *Angle of Repose*
tells a young friend, a college-age woman in the throes of
desultory revolt: "Civilizations grow by agreements and accom-
modations and accretions, not by repudiations. . . . If revolutionaries would learn that they can't remodel society by day
after tomorrow—haven't the wisdom to and shouldn't be per-
mitted to—I'd have more respect for them. . . . Civilizations
grow and change and decline—they aren't remade."[3] I do not
share fully this character's quietude—a restless quietude, to be
sure. But I take the point. Culture changes through the ongoing engagement between tradition and transformation. If we
lose tradition, there will be no transformation. Only the abyss.

As I write this preface, on a sparkling, windy spring day
in Cambridge, Massachusetts, where I am spending a semester
at Harvard, I have three further preliminary thoughts. The first
is that, having just become a grandmother, I am touched and
elated and saddened. This glorious mark of the passage of
time reminds us of our own mortality. We are being told that,
one day, we must get out of the way to make room for newcomers. And that is as it should be. My sadness does not flow
from that recognition; rather, it wells up as I reflect on the kind
of America my granddaughter will grow up in. Because she
has wonderful parents and a big, supportive family, she has
the best of all possible head starts. But that will not suffice. If

she is to take her place as a proud citizen one day, there must be a culture worthy of endorsement and engagement. I am not convinced that is the America she will discover a mere fifteen or twenty years from now.

Second, I ponder the fate of that world of which I have been a part for two decades, the world of teachers and students and scholars. A person unknown to me, who listened to a lecture I delivered at a New England university, handed me an E-mail message that had come in on his computer. He delivered it to me with some hesitancy, he indicated, but as I was the subject of the message, he thought I should have it. From a professor at the University of Calgary, Canada, to the editor of an American feminist journal, the message was pithy: "I've just read Jean Bethke Elshtain's *Democracy on Trial*, the transcript of her Massey Lectures broadcast on CBC radio (up here in Canada, eh). I was surprised by her perspective, which seemed liberal in the classical sense. Is she considered an apostate from academic feminism? Are her books considered suitable for WMST classrooms?" End of message, startling in its severity and its brevity.

What most interested me was the breezy use of the language of apostasy; the unself-conscious endorsement of and search for guidance on the interdiction of a text, preventing its use as "unsuitable" for women's studies courses. Dare one put a book described as "classically liberal" in the hands of students in such a classroom? How astonishing that some among us whose tacit Hippocratic oath commits them to thoroughness and fairness in inquiry do not even bother to hide this sort of thing anymore. Instead, we seek instructions on just how suppressive we ought to be as a kind of pedagogical duty. The implications of this moralistic attitude ("I'm a child of light. Is she a child of

darkness?") are pretty clear. The academy has *not* been over-
taken by this sort of thing, not by a long shot, but there are
determined claques who would move us in that direction.

Finally, I write two days after the death of President
Richard M. Nixon. Back in the good old bad days of the 1970s,
I was second to none as a Nixon loather, and I stayed glued to
the radio and television, lapping up the investigation of Water-
gate as a starving cat does milk. I was therefore surprised at
my own reaction to his passing. Reading Frank Rich's column
in the *New York Times* helped me to understand my reaction.
Rich wrote, "For an American who came of age with him in
the second half of the 20th century, making peace with
Richard Nixon proved in the end an essential part of growing
up."[4] By the time this book is published, Nixon's death will
have been absorbed into wider streams and currents of my life
and that of my country. I mention it because, in his own way,
this complex man, humiliated and disgraced, struggled for the
last two decades of his life to regain a measure of respect from
his fellow citizens. If we no longer create in America men and
women who can be shamed and made to pay a price for dis-
honoring the public trust, but who, in turn, strive to recover
just a few moments of civic grace, we will have lost a culture
that is strong enough to censure presidents and kind enough
to permit them to recover their dignity through civil accomplishment. I am somewhat abashed now as I look back twenty
years or more and recognize how easy it was for me to hate. I
do not hate anymore. I have joined the ranks of the nervous.

Cambridge, Massachusetts
April 24, 1994

DEMOCRACY ON TRIAL

1

Democracy's Precarious Present

WE are blessed, or cursed, to live in interesting times. Even as the nations and peoples formerly under the domination of the Soviet Union proclaim their political ideals in language that inspired and secured the founding of Western democracies, and even as Russia and the various successor states that have sprung up in the wreckage of the terrible Soviet system flail toward democracy or run away from it, our American democracy is faltering. In this first chapter, I explore warning signs of exhaustion, cynicism, opportunism, and despair using the American experiment as my chief example of the troubles to which democracy is prey. The trials and tribulations of the American republic have a way of setting the agenda for other democratic societies—for better or for worse, and no doubt some of both.

The signs of the times are not encouraging. To interpret those signs is not easy, unless one reacts automatically from a stance of harsh ideological predetermination, whether of the Left or the Right. Let me begin with a few general considerations that flow from the preoccupations of democratic thinkers, past and present. A major concern for all who care about democracy is the everyday actions and spirit of a people. Democracy requires laws, constitutions, and authoritative institutions, yes, but it also depends on what might be called democratic dispositions. These include a preparedness to work with others different from oneself toward shared ends; a combination of strong convictions with a readiness to compromise in the recognition that one can't always get everything one wants; and a sense of individuality and a commitment to civic goods that are not the possession of one person or of one small group alone. But what do we see when we look around? We find deepening cynicism; the growth of corrosive forms of isolation, boredom, and despair; the weakening, in other words, of that world known as democratic civil society, a world of groups and associations and ties that bind.

Many political commentators in the United States have written of the growth of a "culture of mistrust," aided by scandals, a press that feeds off scandals, and a public whose appetite for scandals seems insatiable. The culture of mistrust fuels declining levels of involvement in politics and stokes cynicism about politics and politicians. Journalist E. J. Dionne's book *Why Americans Hate Politics* offers an account of what has gone awry. According to Dionne, both liberals and conservatives are failing America. He laments the false polarization in American politics that has been cast in the form of a cultural civil war: Give no quarter! One mark of this divide is the irony of liberals seeking ways to tame the logic of the market in economic life even as they celebrate a nearly untrammeled laissez-faire in cultural and sexual life. Their mirror image is provided by conservatives, who argue for constraints and controls in the cultural and sexual sphere but embrace a nearly unconstrained market.[1] Politicians and citizens get stuck in the *danse macabre* of these two logics and see no clear way out. Needless to say, it is far easier, as Dionne points out, for the media to reinforce the political and cultural divide than to explore ideas that cannot be captured so easily by one logic or the other.

A second perceptive analysis of America's political travail is *Chain Reaction,* an account by Thomas Byrne Edsall and Mary D. Edsall of "the impact of race, rights, and taxes on American politics."[2] The Edsalls describe how numerous programs targeted specifically at black and underclass Americans have lost political legitimacy. Preferential hiring programs, for example, have provoked resentment and have stoked, rather than healed, racial divisions. Various forms of welfare provision seem to encourage out-of-wedlock births: the rate is around 70 percent for inner-city mothers, many of them teenagers, and is growing rapidly for young white teenagers. Dependence on welfare benefits threatens, over time, to lock these young women into what Mary Jo Bane and David Ellwood, members of the Clinton administration's policy staff, have called a "client-compliance culture" that is much at odds with the possibilities for adult citizenship. A "client" who shows some get-up-and-go may find herself categorized as "error prone"—bureaucratic lingo for a welfare recipient who works more than her eligibility rules permit.[3] She becomes an administrative nuisance, rather than a person with spunk.

In an era of declining resources, resentments cluster around government-sponsored efforts that do not seem to solve the problems they were designed to solve (as voters were told when they signed on to the social contract to make provision for those less fortunate). That is, citizens who pay most of the bills no longer see a benefit flowing from such programs to the society as a whole. Instead, they see a growing dependence on welfare, increased inner-city crime, an epidemic of out-of-wedlock births, and the like. They perceive, therefore, a pattern of redistribution through forms of assistance to people who do not seem to be as committed as they are to following the rules of the game by working hard and not expecting the government to shoulder their burdens. This, at least, is the widespread conviction, and it fuels popular anger and perplexity. As a result, programs geared to particular populations have lost the legitimacy accorded almost automatically to inclusive programs such as social security. Despite their unpopularity, policies that target particular groups are difficult to alter once they are in place, given the phenomenon called "clientele capture." This term refers to the small number of vocal "clients" of such policies—most often the middle-class bureaucrats who administer the programs rather than aid recipients themselves—who have a vested interest in preventing change, even though, over the long run, a policy loses the support of the vast majority of citizens.

The problem goes even deeper than the apparent intractable nature of what Bane and Ellwood called the "basic culture of the welfare system," one that relies on people being weak and having their "needs" defined for them by others. Consider, for example, the working poor who do not flout the rules, try to hold their families together, and are often too proud to ask for assistance even if they may be eligible. Ironically, they are currently the poorest of the poor, severed from the service- and cash-based forms of aid available to those on welfare. These people, hundreds of thousands of our fellow citizens, are finding themselves in increasingly desperate straits as low-paying jobs shrink and wages stagnate. These are people who play by the rules yet appear to be losing nonetheless. This makes it much more difficult to hold up the civic virtues of sobriety, rectitude, hard work, and familial and community responsibility.

DEMOCRATIC CIVIL SOCIETY

These and other examples of disaffection, including that heart of darkness evoked by American youths from social worlds that are by no means "unprivileged," speak to a deeper matter. As a *civic* question—and it is by no means a civic matter alone—the locus of despair speaks to the loss of civil society. This deepening emptiness, a kind of evacuation of civic spaces, lies in the background of our current discontents, helping to explain why democracy is going through an ordeal of self-understanding as we near the end of the twentieth century. In the associational enthusiasms of civil society, the democratic ethos and spirits of citizens are made manifest. By *civil society,* I mean the many forms of community and association that dot the landscape of a democratic culture, from families to churches to neighborhood groups to trade unions to self-help movements to volunteer assistance to the needy. Historically, political parties, too, were a robust part of this picture. This network lies outside the formal structure of state power. Observers of democracy have long recognized the vital importance of civil society. Some have spoken of "mediating institutions" that lie between the individual and the government or state. These mediating institutions located the child, for example, in his or her little estate, the family, which was itself nested within a wider, overlapping framework of sustaining and supporting civic institutions: churches, schools, and solidaristic organizations, such as unions or mothers' associations. American society was honeycombed by a vast network that offered a densely textured social ecology for the growing citizen.

Curiously, the framers of the American Constitution paid little explicit attention to such institutions, including the family. Perhaps they did not do so because they simply assumed that these associations of civil society were vital and would be long-lasting. They counted on a social deposit of intergenerational trust, neighborliness, and civic responsibility. But we no longer can. That is why political theorists, of whom I am one, must tend explicitly to this matter. We see the ill effects of the loss of civil society all around us.

Think, if you will and if you can bear it, of the growing number of American children for whom not home nor street nor neighborhood affords a safe haven. American children are growing up frightened, and an increasing number of them are being scarred by violence in the schools and streets. The data are overwhelming and consistent. We know that the strongest predictors of domestic situations in which children are likely to be physically abused are stressed-out single-parent households with a teenaged mother, often of several children, and households consisting of a biological mother and her children living with a man who is not related to those children or who does not accept legal responsibility for their well-being. Undersupervised foster care is another recipe for potential disaster; why should this surprise us? These are situations that have been stripped of a dense *sociality*, situations in which the outer world—sometimes that means just outside the door of one's apartment—undermines even the most mature and responsible parents. We further know that a stable, two-parent household is the best protection not only against child abuse but against the possibility that a child will grow up to be an abuser. Again, why should this surprise us? Those who take public responsibility for their stewardship of a private world are more likely to be held accountable and to hold themselves accountable. They are more likely to be sustained by a network of helpful "others"—neighbors, relatives, or associations of all kinds, formal and informal.

Fully 70 percent of juveniles in state reform institutions grew up in homes with a severe "parental deficit," as the sociologists like to call it. I refer to domestic circumstances with fewer helping hands than necessary and less than adequate emotional, economic, and social support. Beyond the tragedy of children assaulted in their homes, an astonishing number die from violence—especially from guns. Homicide by firearms is now the third leading cause of death for fifteen- to nineteen-year-old white Americans (after motor vehicle accidents and suicide). For black Americans in the same age bracket, homicide is the leading cause of death. Why do we tolerate that decimation of African American young people and the sad fact that the suicide rate among young white men has jumped over 200 percent in the past decade? Young white men, aged fifteen to nineteen, are in more danger of self-destruction than any other group. There is more: The prime determinant of drinking or drug use is how many hours a child is left alone during the week. Over the long run, stemming the tide of family collapse is the best protection we can offer a child against becoming either the victim or the perpetrator of violence—or, as it turns out, of poverty.[4]

Seventy-nine percent of children whose parents are unmarried, did not complete high school, and had a first child before age twenty wind up in poverty. Only 8 percent of children with married parents who completed high school and waited until age twenty to bear a child are poor. In other words, married parents who are not high school dropouts are a child's best protection against both poverty and violence.[5] But families cannot do this alone. They need neighbors to turn to; churches to give not only solace but solid, hands-on help; a network of friends; and agencies that assist in time of trouble, such as a serious, prolonged illness. That socially rich world is the world of civil society. If we are to sustain our democratic culture, we must depend on that world. It is not surprising that in areas where the social fabric has most thoroughly come unraveled, we see the most dire and distressing evidence of violence, neglect, babies having babies, desperate grandparents whose children are lost to them trying to raise grandchildren, and all the rest. Neither is it surprising that 67 percent of black adults believe their families and churches will help black families the most, or that only 14 percent believe the government can weave together the warp and woof of their communities at risk. They continue to place their ever more fragile hope in the possibility of civil society.

Civil society is a realm that is neither individualist nor collectivist. It partakes of both the "I" and the "we." Here I think of the many lodges and clubs and party precinct organizations that once dotted the American landscape. It is that world of small-scale social and civic bodies that the Anti-Federalists evoked in debates over ratification of the United States Constitution. The Anti-Federalists were not as confident as the Federalists about the long-term survival of robust civic bodies, and they hoped to ensure that these bodies would flourish. No doubt these Anti-Federalists pushed an idealized image of a self-reliant republic that shunned imperial power and worked, instead, to create a polity modeled on classic principles of civic virtue and the common good. As Ralph Ketcham, a historian of this argument, wrote: "Anti-federalists saw mild, grass-roots, small-scale governments in sharp contrast to the splendid edifice and overweening ambitions implicit in the new Constitution. . . . The first left citizens free to live their own lives and to cultivate the virtue (private and public) vital to republicanism, while the second soon entailed taxes and drafts and offices and wars damaging to human dignity and thus fatal to self-government."[6]

Despite the often roseate hue with which the Anti-Federalists surrounded their arguments, they were on to something, as we like to say. They hoped to avoid, even to break, a cycle later elaborated by Alexis de Tocqueville in his great nineteenth-century work, *Democracy in America*. Tocqueville sketched as a warning a world in decline, a world different from the robust democracy he surveyed. He believed that American democratic citizens needed to take to heart a possible corruption of their way of life. In his worst-

case scenario, narrowly self-interested individualists, disartic-
ulated from the saving constraints and nurture of overlapping
associations of social life, would require more and more controls "from above" to mute at least somewhat the disintegra-
tive effects of individualism of a narrowly egoistic sort.

To this end, he cautioned, the peripheries must remain
vital; political spaces other than or beneath those of the state
need to be cherished, nourished, and kept vibrant. Tocqueville
had in mind local councils and committees, to forestall con-
centrations of power at the core or on the top. Too much centralized power is as bad as no power, he believed. Only many
small-scale civic bodies would enable citizens to cultivate
democratic virtues and to play an active role in the drama of
democracy. Such participation turns on meaningful involvement in some form of community. Too much power exercised
at a level beyond that which permits and encourages active citizen participation is destructive of civic dignity and may prove
fatal to democratic self-government. We see, then, that early
Anti-Federalist fears of centralized power presaged Tocqueville's uneasy premonition that imperial greatness bought
through force of arms is "pleasing to the imagination of a
democratic people" because it sends out lightning bolts of
"vivid and sudden luster, obtained without toil, by nothing but
the risk of life."[7] This latter course is, despite the expenditure
of blood and treasure it requires, far easier than tending to the
daily work of democratic civic life.

Tocqueville's worries have been much debated by political and social theorists. Those who follow Tocqueville in
this matter believe that American democracy did free individuals from the constraints of older, undemocratic structures

and obligations. But, at the same time, it unleashed an individualism of a peculiarly cramped sort. Tocqueville's fear, remember, was not that this development would invite anarchy—as antidemocratic philosophers claim or insist—but that the individualism of an acquisitive commercial republic would engender new forms of social and political domination. He called this bad form of individualism "egoism," to distinguish it from the notions of human dignity and self-responsibility central to a flourishing democratic way of life. All social webs that once held persons intact having disintegrated, the individual finds himself or herself isolated and impotent, exposed and unprotected. Into this power vacuum will likely move a top-heavy, ever more centralized state. Or we will hunker down in defensive "lifestyle enclaves," forbidding others entry. As political theorist Michael Walzer noted:

> We are perhaps the most individualist society that ever existed in human history. Compared certainly to earlier, and Old World societies, we are radically liberated, all of us. Free to plot our own course. To plan our own lives. To choose a career. To choose a partner or a succession of partners. To choose a religion or no religion. To choose a politics or an anti-politics. To choose a lifestyle—any style. Free to do our own thing, and this freedom, energizing and exciting as it is, is also profoundly disintegrative, making it very difficult for individuals to find any stable communal support, very difficult for any community to count on the responsible participation of its individual members. It opens solitary men and women to the impact of a lowest common denominator, commercial culture. It works against commitment to the

larger democratic union and also against the solidarity of
all cultural groups that constitute our multi-culturalism.[8]

Keep in mind the concern that over time the stripping
down of the individual to a hard core of an isolated or a sus-
pended self, the celebration of a version of radical autonomy,
casts suspicion on any and all ties of reciprocal obligation and
mutual interdependence. What counts in this scheme of things
is the individual and his or her choices. If choice is made
absolute, it follows that important and troubling questions that
arise as one evaluates the distinction between individual right
and social obligation are blanked out of existence. One simply
gives everything, or nearly so, over to the individualist pole in
advance. Ideally, democratic individuality is "not boundless
subjectivist or self-seeking individualism," but the worry is that
it has, over time, become so.[9] The blessings of democratic life
that Tocqueville so brilliantly displayed—especially the spirit
of equality, including a certain informality and mixing of peoples of different stations—give way. In their place, other more
fearful and self-enclosed, more suspicious and cynical habits
and dispositions rise to the fore. We cannot stand isolated for
long in the wind with no protective cover. Ironically, the individualism sketched here erodes the possibility of democratic
freedom over time, the blessings of liberty to ourselves and
our posterity.

In his book *The True and Only Heaven,* historian and cultural critic Christopher Lasch told the tale this way. In the eighteenth century, the founders of modern liberalism embraced
an argument that posited human wants and needs as expand-
able—indeed, nearly insatiable. It followed that indefinite

growth of the productive forces of economic life was needed to satisfy and continually fuel the restless cycle of the creation and satiation of needs. This ideology, called Progress, was distinctive, Lasch claimed, in exempting its world from the judgment of time and led to the unqualified and altogether unwarranted optimism that a way of life could persist untarnished, undamaged, and without terrible pressure to its own, most cherished principles.[10]

The joint property of various liberalisms and conservatisms, twentieth-century purveyors of progress as an ideology celebrated a world of endless growth, which meant, in practice, more and better consumerism. It was essential to move from the glorification of producer to the glorification of the consumer because the conclusion was that underconsumption leads to declining investment. We want more, and we want it now! All of life is invaded by the market and pervaded by market imagery. Perhaps we should not be too surprised that in America's inner cities, young people rob, beat, and even kill one another to steal expensive sneakers and gold chains. Or that in America's suburbs, young people whose families are well off shun school and studies and community involvement to take part-time jobs to pay for extra consumer goods that their parents may be loath to provide.

I take Lasch's argument to be similar to Pope John Paul II's criticism of "liberal capitalism" in "Sollicitudo Rei Socialis," his encyclical on social concerns. Rejecting the self-contained smugness of the ideology of Progress, John Paul scored a phenomenon he called "superdevelopment, which consists in an excessive availability of every kind of material good for the benefit of certain social groups." Superdevelopment "makes people slaves of 'possession' and of immediate gratification, with no other horizon than the multiplication or continual replacement of the things already owned with others still better. This is the so-called civilization of 'consumption' or 'consumerism,' which involves so much 'throwing away' and 'waste.'"[11]

The "sad effects of this blind submission to pure consumerism," John Paul stated, are a combination of materialism and restless dissatisfaction as the "more one possesses the more one wants." Aspirations that cut deeper, that speak to human dignity within a world of others, are stifled. John Paul's name for this alternative aspiration is "solidarity," not "a feeling of vague compassion or shallow distress at the misfortunes of so many people" but a determination to "commit oneself to the common good; that is to say, to the good of all and of each individual because we are really responsible for all." Through solidarity, John Paul said, we *see* "the 'other' . . . not just as some kind of instrument . . . but as our 'neighbor,' a 'helper' . . . to be made a sharer on a par with ourselves in the banquet of life to which all are equally invited by God."[12]

To the extent that John Paul's words strike us as utopian or naive, we have lost civil society. Or so, at least, sociologist Alan Wolfe concluded in *Whose Keeper? Social Science and Moral Obligation.* Wolfe updated Tocqueville, apprising us of how far and how rapidly we have traveled down the road to bad individualism, which requires the greater management, control, and concentration of political and economic power to keep us bounded in our little kingdoms of one. Wolfe suggested that for all our success in modern societies, there is a sense, desperate in some cases, that all is not well, that something has gone terribly awry. We citizens of liberal democratic societies understand and cherish our freedom, but we are, according to Wolfe, "confused when it comes to recognizing the social obligations that make . . . freedom possible in the first place."[13] This confusion permeates all levels, from the marketplace to the home to the academy.

The confusion has a lot to do with a new attitude toward rights that has taken hold in the United States during the past several decades. Americans have been speaking the language of rights for a long time. It is part of our heritage, as American as apple pie. The first noticeable mention of rights, the Bill of Rights, was appended to, and became part of, the American Constitution. These rights revolve around civic freedoms— assembly, press, speech—and around what the government cannot do to you, say, unreasonable search and seizure. Rights were designed primarily as immunities, as a way to protect us from overweening governmental power, not as entitlements. The rights-bearing individual was a civic creature, a commu- nity being, a family man or woman located within the world of civil society I have already described. But as time passed, the rights-bearing individual came to stand alone—"me and my rights"—as if rights were a possession. Rights were construed increasingly in individualistic terms as their civic dimensions withered on the vine. As legal theorist Mary Ann Glendon pointed out in her book *Rights Talk*, the dimensions of social- ity and responsibility are missing when the rights-defined self stands alone.[14] The regime of rights cannot be sustained by rights alone.

These ideas help us make sense of the political fallout from "rights talk" that surely puts democracy on trial. Let me elaborate by further developing one of my earlier claims. On the one hand, we witness a morally exhausted Left embracing the logic of the market by endorsing the translation of *wants* into *rights*. Although the political Left continues to argue for taming the market in an economic sense, it follows the market model when social relations are concerned, seeing in any restriction of individual "freedom" or "lifestyle option," as we call it today, an unacceptable diminution of rights and free expression. On the other hand, many on the political Right love the untrammeled (or the less trammeled the better) operations of the market in economic life, but call for a state-enforced restoration of traditional mores, including strict sexual and social scripts for men and women in family and work life. Both rely on either the market or the state to "organize their codes of moral obligation, but what they really need," Wolfe insisted, "is civil society—families, communities, friendship networks, solidaristic workplace ties, voluntarism, spontaneous groups and movements—not to reject, but to complete the project of modernity."[15]

What is needed to speed this cherished end—the revivification of civil society—is a return to a more thoroughly social understanding that rights are always transitive, always involve us with others, cannot stand alone, and cannot come close to exhausting who and what we are. If we were to try to understand through "rights talk" why we stay up all night with a sick child or take our neighbor a pot of soup when she comes home from the hospital or spend hours helping to provide for the victims of a natural disaster, we would seriously distort these socially responsible and compassionate activities. We know this in our bones. Yet each time we feel called upon to justify something politically, we tend to make our concerns far more individualistic and asocial than they really are by reverting to the language of rights as the "first language" of liberal democracy.[16]

None of the thinkers I have mentioned has found a solution to our Tocquevillian anxiety in a more powerful state, including the welfare state as we know it. The most highly developed welfare state in nineteenth-century Europe was Bismarck's "welfare-warfare" state, one in which social benefits were geared explicitly to making the poor loyal dependents of the state. Social control was the aim, welfare the strategy. For most of us in the modern West, the welfare state emerged from a set of ethical concerns and passions that grew as civil society began to succumb to market forces. These concerns ushered in the conviction that the state was the "only agent capable of serving as a surrogate for the moral ties of civil society." But half a century of evidence makes it clear that the logic of the state's provision and creation of classes of long-term dependents in America has further eroded "the very social ties that make government possible in the first place."[17]

Please note well: The argument behind "ending welfare as we know it," when it comes from the direction of a civil society, is not about grinding the faces of the poor into dust from a lack of compassion. Rather, it is about how welfare professionalizes care and counsel and turns citizens into clients. In "Community and Its Counterfeits," a series aired on the Canadian Broadcasting Corporation (CBC), John McKnight, scholar and community activist, claimed that modern institutions are machines that redefine human beings, locating us as entities in a system, rather than as people in a place. When professionals move in on communities to "solve a problem," what happens is that people grow weaker, not stronger, for their "needs" are authoritatively defined by sources outside themselves. The "awakened energies of the community are often dissipated in a maze of government regulations or resources are tied up in social programs which deliver services to people whose real need is income," McKnight argued.

Needs, then, become "the resources of the service sector of contemporary economies—what iron ore is to the steel industry, needs are to those who propose to meet them." According to McKnight, this "never-ending search for new needs . . . is always at the cost of diminished citizenship. So that as these systems of service colonize your life and my life, saying that we are bundles of needs and there are institutionalized services there to meet the needs to make us whole, to make us real, what we become is less and less powerful."

I am not so naive or foolish as to believe we can do without the state. The state, properly chastened, plays a vital role in a democratic society. Rather, I am worried about the *logic* of statism, which looks to the state as the only entity capable of "solving a problem" or responding to a concern. One problem with this logic is that as the state expands its role, the capacities of local institutions are often diminished. Another is what may be called the *ideology* of statism, which is not as prevalent in North American democracy as it was in the civic republican polities imagined by Jean-Jacques Rousseau and implemented in the early-modern and modern epochs by various civic actors, beginning with the French Revolutionaries in the eighteenth century.

The statist wants to thin out the ties of civil society and to erode the force of the plural loyalties and diverse imperatives these ties give rise to and sustain. To the statist, the citizen is unhesitatingly loyal to the state and is prepared to give primacy to it and its purposes. The statist identifies us—we citizens—primarily as creatures who are available for mobilization by a powerful centralized mechanism, rather than as family members, neighbors, participants in a fraternal order or a feminist health cooperative, activists trying to save the African elephant from extinction, members of a reading group, Baptists, Catholics, and so on. The statist wants us to be hemmed in and obliged and homogenized in all sorts of mandated ways.

But the citizen of a democratic civil society understands that government cannot substitute for concrete moral obligations; it can either deplete or nourish them. As our sense of particular, morally grounded responsibilities to an intergenerational web and a world of friends and neighbors falters and the state moves in to treat the dislocations, it may temporarily solve delimited problems. But these solutions may, in time, further thin out the skein of obligation. Eventually, support for the state itself will begin to plummet—people feel anomic and aggrieved, their resentments swell—and one sees the evidence in tax evasion; an upsurge in violence against persons and property; the breakup of social ties, including families, on an unprecedented scale; the rise of political cynicism; and even something akin to despair.

A number of contemporary observers, including several I have already cited, see such signs of civic and social trouble even in the long-established welfare democracies of Western Europe and Scandinavia. It is, alas, the by now familiar story: the loneliness of the aged, the apathy of the young, the withering away of churches and communal organizations, the disentangling of family ties, and the loss of family rituals and rhythms. I do not want to say that the provision of welfare directly caused any of these phenomena. I do want to suggest that a bureaucratic, top-heavy state that numbers among its tasks defining populations by their "needs" and targeting them for various policies based on assumptions about such needs, really cannot help moving in the direction of a "social engineering" that exists in tension with democratic freedom, civic sociality, and individual liberty.

No doubt a distinction should be made between the dominant rhetoric of individualism and the culture of cynicism, on the one hand, and how we actually behave as members of families, communities, churches, and neighborhoods, on the other. But surely it is true that our social practices are under extraordinary pressure and thus that democracy itself is being squeezed. In America today, fearful people rush to arm themselves, believing safety to be a matter of aggressive self-help. Angry people want all the politicians to be kicked out of office, but they believe new ones will be no better. Anxious people fear that their neighbors' children may get some unfair advantage over their own. Despairing people destroy their own lives and the lives of those around them. Careless people ignore their children and then blast the teachers and social workers who must tend to the mess they have made, screaming all the while that folks ought to "mind their own business." Many human ills cannot be cured, of course. All human lives are lived on the edge of quiet desperation. We must all be rescued from time to time from fear and sorrow. But I read the palpable despair and cynicism and violence as dark signs of the times, as warnings that democracy may not be up to the task of satisfying the yearnings it unleashes for freedom and fairness and equality.

"DEFINING DEVIANCY DOWN"

I spend a lot of time talking to young people, going from campus to campus giving lectures. In April 1994, I gave a talk at a fine institution a good two-and-a-half-hour drive from the nearest airport. Those who fetched me at the airport and returned me there later that day were students. They told me they had no really clear ideas about what lay ahead or what they wanted to be. I was struck by one bright young man, who was perturbed by the recent suicide of Kurt Cobain, front man for the group Nirvana, considered the band that best embodies "Generation X." This student said—and, remember, he is among the privileged—that his generation is cynical: "If you have a thought that doesn't seem cynical, you have to get cynical about your own noncynicism, so you can be safely cynical again and not seem like a dweeb or optimist of some sort." He hailed from a volatile private world of once-feuding parents, then a "broken home"—his words, not mine. He was thoughtful but all at sea, and he envied earlier generations because they seemed to have "purpose." I told him I thought it was not so much "purpose" as that we middle-aged folks grew up with adult examples of steadiness, competence, and integrity and that these models were fast disappearing. It was a sobering drive.

Let us take a closer look. Counsels of despair are of little help and all too easily descend into bathos and even self-indulgence. One sign that democracy is on trial is the falling away from the firm, buoyant conviction of democrats that a rights-based democratic equality, guaranteed by the vote, will serve over time as the sure and secure basis of a democratic culture. Political theorist George Kateb, for example, celebrates "democratic individuality," reflected in and protected by "the electoral procedure, the set of rules" that embody the "great value of equal respect for persons." Such rules, including the franchise as a right, radiate "a strong influence" that goes much beyond the formal prerogatives themselves, helping to instill a sense of dignity and permanently chastening political authority should it grow overweening.[18] Kateb does well to remind us of the distinction between destructive individualism and the ennobling strengths of the democratic tradition of respect for the human person, taken as a single, unique, and irreplaceable self.

But a striking feature of our epoch is that those very rights, the terms of democratic equality itself, have fallen into disrepute. Rather than rights serving as a frame within which democratic individuality can be shored up—in which a self is made possible by the debates and dialogues a rule-governed democratic culture sustains—we hear ever more cynical appraisals of the rules, regulations, procedures, guarantees, and premises of constitutional democracy. For example, fueled by claims that wildly exaggerate the extent of violence perpetrated against women—for the media's hysteria knows no restraint in this matter—various proposals have been made based on the premise that burdensome democratic procedures, including the presumption of innocence, should be seen for what they are: bourgeois hypocrisy. We should recognize that the presumption of innocence and the need for our accusers to bear the burden of proof will protect us and our loved ones if we are ever called before the bar of justice; instead, we are bombarded with arguments belittling, even trashing, the whole idea of evidentiary requirements that are central to the ideal of equal standing before the law.

This short temper with honoring the rights of the accused and meting out punishment appropriate to fit the concrete, particular crime that may have occurred is powerfully evident in a piece of legislation up for passage in the U.S. Senate. It represents a danger to democratic ideas of fairness and due process and embodies a mind-set that will be around for some time. Called the Violence Against Women Act, the legislation incorporates "gender motivation" into a law that presumes to see in rape—a crime of violence—the paradigmatic, indeed normative, expression of male dominance. This act is an example of what Senator Daniel Patrick Moynihan called "defining deviancy down," on the legislative front in this instance. What is aberrant is suddenly redescribed as normal. Thus one moves away from the guiding presumptions of democratic jurisprudence, namely, that each case must be looked at individually: one must assess what happened to this victim and what was perpetrated by that offender. Instead, the defenders of this new approach assume an undifferentiated class of victimizers (male) of an undifferentiated class of victims (female), raising the specter that the concrete facts in a case of sexual assault will be much less important in establishing guilt or innocence than will some vague "animus based on a victim's gender." The motive police here rely on the platitudes of radical feminist ideology, a view of the moral and social world that, in the words of Catharine MacKinnon, "stresses the indistinguishability of prostitution, marriage, and sexual harassment."[19] In this scheme of things, sex is what men do *to* women. It follows that men simply *are* rapists, either actual or in situ. What is lost is the truth expressed by our new Supreme Court Justice, Ruth Bader Ginsburg, that "generalizations about the way women or men are . . . cannot guide me reliably in making decisions about particular individuals."[20] One finds, then, at this moment, the distressing spectacle of an assault on civil liberties, coupled with a perfervid ideology of victimization.[21]

Political philosopher Charles Taylor rightly noted the tremendous amount of activity that is discernible in American politics, an incessant hubbub, as a matter of fact, but he described the American political scene as dismal, in part because American society has grown ever more fragmented: "A fragmented society is one whose members find it harder and harder to identify with their political society as a community. This lack of identification may reflect an atomistic outlook, in which people come to see society purely instrumentally. But it also helps to entrench atomism, because the absence of effective common action throws people back on themselves."[22] We are thrown back on ourselves, into the currents of consumer excess or the cold comfort of ever more computerized and centralized bureaucracies.

I think of the words now used to characterize American politics: stalemate, gridlock, cynicism. American politics is a miasma, so argue many experts and journalists, as well as ordinary citizens. This growing cynicism about politics promotes a spiral of delegitimation. How does a spiral of delegitimation get a society in its grip? Over time, the "culture of mistrust" grows, aided, as I already indicated, by public scandals; by an ever more litigious and suspicious society; by a determination to "get mine" no matter what may happen to the other guy; and by salacious snooping into the private lives of public figures, which further fuels cynicism about how untrustworthy our leaders are even as we delight in their downfall.[23]

It is quite a mess, but it is not America's mess alone. Perhaps it is worth noting that the growth of American cynicism about democratic government shifts America toward, not away from, a more generalized norm of disaffection. Most people in other societies, including citizens of the democracies of Western Europe, are cynical about government. As political scientist James Q. Wilson pointed out, we Americans "are less optimistic and less trusting than we once were. And rightly so: if Washington says that we should entrust it to educate our children, to protect our environment, and to regulate our economy, we would be foolish not to be cautious and skeptical."[24] The problem, according to Wilson, is that over the past three to four decades, government has become less effective, not so much as a result of its size per se, but because it has taken on more and more issues that it is simply ill equipped to handle well—including abortion and race relations, to name two of the most volatile.

Too many such "wedge issues," as the pundits and strategists call them, were created not for the most part by cynical demagogues but by well-meaning federal judges who made decisions in the 1960s and 1970s on a whole range of cultural questions without due consideration of how public support for juridically mandated outcomes might be generated. On some questions—for example, school desegregation—the moral mandate was high and consistent with our own perduring principles. For the Supreme Court to come down decisively on one side of the question led to a fierce political struggle, to be sure, but the whole weight of American history since the Civil War has been behind the commitment to inclusion and equality. Many "cultural" and "ethical" matters are not as clear, however.

Dealing with abortion, to take one example of a controversial ethical and cultural issue, cannot be compared to building a great interstate highway system or desegregating the schools. All the cultural questions that now pit democratic citizens against one another—in addition to abortion, I think of family values, drugs, and post–civil rights race relations—are guaranteed to continue to divide us, in large part because of the means government has often used to put these issues on the table: judicial fiat. The Supreme Court decision in the deeply contentious *Roe v. Wade* case in 1973 actually preempted a nationwide political debate over abortion, then raging in most states. A grass-roots politics to liberalize abortion laws was well under way. Indeed, some sixteen states had already reformed their abortion statutes to make abortion more widely available. In addition, as historian Michael Barone has pointed out, "by the time the *Roe v. Wade* decision was issued, about 70% of the nation's population lived within 100 miles— an easy two hours' drive—of a state with a legalized abortion law. And just as the Supreme Court was speaking, legislatures in almost all of the states were going into session; many would probably have liberalized their abortion laws if the court had not acted."[25]

Regardless of one's personal views on abortion, this case is a good example of juridical moves freezing out citizen debate. Juridical politics is black and white, winner-take-all. The juridical model of politics, first pushed by liberal activists and now embraced by their conservative counterparts—for two can play at this game—preempts democratic contestation and a politics of respect and melioration. When the Supreme Court threw all its weight to one side in a highly fraught situation on which people of goodwill differed, it aroused from the beginning strong and shocked opposition from those who despaired that their government, at its highest level, sanctioned what they took to be the destruction of human life at its most vulnerable stage. By guaranteeing that the forces on either side of the issue need not debate with each other, other than through judges, the court deepened a politics of resentment.

DEMOCRACY BY PLEBISCITE?

There are, alas, many more examples of this sort. Rather than weary the reader with further recounting of such tales, I will look, instead, at a few proposed solutions and assess whether they promise democratic renewal. A direct, rather than a representative, democratic system is one panacea sought by some who are impatient with the compromises and mediations of democratic civil society and frustrated by governmental inaction or too much action of a sort they oppose. Let the people speak! This populist theme is a recurring refrain in American political life. Historically, populists usually wanted government off their backs and power restored to their own communities. Currently, populists—or those who call themselves such—feed on mistrust and antielitism, and anyone who is unlucky enough to hold any kind of governmental office is subject to their ire.

In the American presidential election of 1992, populist fervor gained surprising strength in the person, and candidacy, of the Texas billionaire Ross Perot. Perot is far less important than the phenomenon he helped to catalyze. Consider, briefly, one of his proposed cures for democratic ills, a cure that has been endorsed, to ends rather different from Mr. Perot's, by some commentators on the Left. Such populists, or strong democrats as they like to be called, would perfect democracy by eliminating barriers between the people's will and its forthright articulation. Pure democracy beckons, whirring and humming in the background of such visions, sometimes called the electronic town hall.

American democracy is in trouble, the proponents of pure democracy believe, because the direct expression of the people's will is thwarted. But technology will come to our rescue through instant plebiscites via interactive television and telepolling. Should we include managed competition in a health-care proposal? Press the yes button or the no button. Should we bomb Baghdad because of yet another blunder or nefarious scheme by Saddam Hussein? Choose your button. What those who push such technosolutions fail to appreciate is that plebiscitary majoritarianism is quite different from a democratic polity sustained by debate and judgment. Plebiscites have been used routinely to shore up antidemocratic regimes—Argentinian Peronism comes to mind.

Even if one could devise a way to "sample" the political responses of America's 120 million households, the plebiscite solution to democratic disillusionment must be criticized no matter who is championing its use. The distinction between a democratic and a plebiscitary system is no idle one. In a plebiscitary system, the views of the majority can more easily swamp minority or unpopular views. Plebiscitarianism is compatible with authoritarian politics carried out under the guise of, or with the connivance of, majority opinion. That opinion can be registered ritualistically, so there is no need for debate with one's fellow citizens on substantive questions. All that is required is a calculus of opinion.

True democracy, Abraham Lincoln's "last, best hope on earth," is a different proposition. It requires a mode of participation with one's fellow citizens that is animated by a sense of responsibility for one's society. The participation of plebiscitarianism is dramatically at odds with this democratic ideal. Watching television and pushing a button are privatizing experiences; they appeal to us as consumers, not as public citizens.

Being asked your opinion and given a chance to register it instantly may at first seem democratic, but the individual in this formulation is the private person enclosed within herself or himself, rather than the public citizen. A compilation of opinions does not make a civic culture; such a culture emerges only from a deliberative process. To see button-pressing as a meaningful act on a par with lobbying, meeting, writing letters to the editor, serving on the local school board, working for a candidate, or helping to forge a coalition to promote or prevent a particular program or policy parallels a crude version of so-called preference theory in economics.

This theory holds that in a free-market society, the sum total of individual consumer choices results in the greatest benefit to society as a whole even as these choices meet individual needs. The assumption is that each of us is a "preference maximizer." Aside from being a simplistic account of human motivation, preference theory lends itself to the blurring of important distinctions. According to preference maximizers, there is no such thing as a social good—there are only aggregates of private goods. Measuring our opinions through electronic town halls is a variant of this crude but common notion. The cure it promises is more of what ails us. Under the banner of a perfected democratic choice, we become complicit in eroding even further those elements of deliberation, reason, judgment, and shared goodwill that alone make genuine choice, hence democracy, possible. We would turn our representatives into factotums, mouthpieces expressing our electronically generated will. This is a nightmare, not a democratic dream.

A NEW SOCIAL COVENANT?

Is there any way to break the spiral of mistrust and cynicism? Yes, but it will be difficult. Some, and I include myself in this number, embrace the idea of a new social covenant. But unless Americans, or the citizens of any faltering democracy, can once again be shown that they are all in it together; unless democratic citizens remember that being a citizen is a *civic* identity, not primarily a private sinecure; unless government can find a way to respond to people's deepest concerns, a new democratic social covenant has precious little chance of taking hold. And take hold it must if we are to stem the tide of divisive issues that pit citizen against citizen in what social scientists call a zero-sum game: I win; you lose—that juridical model of politics I have already decried. The social covenant is not a dream of unanimity or harmony, but the name given to a hope that we can draw on what we hold in common even as we disagree.

Let us imagine how a new social covenant might work in America's troubled cities. It would draw whites and blacks together around their shared concern for safe streets and neighborhoods, in part by altering the terms of the public debate. The social covenantee would encourage liberals who espouse untrammeled lifestyle options to be tolerant of the more conservative values and concerns—especially those of family and religious faith.

The interviews I have conducted with mothers and grandmothers who are active in antigang and antidrug politics in their communities show clearly how much at odds their views are with the dogma that refuses to confront the realities of violence and even chaos in housing projects and on dangerous streets. Social provision will not deal with this problem, one that is overwhelmingly a matter of the deterioration and deinstitutionalization of families, churches, and neighborhoods. These institutions must be rebuilt; in the meantime, the violence must be stopped. The mothers I spoke to want more police patrols, more neighborhood power, less freedom for armed teenagers to run amok, and tougher penalties for repeat offenders.

As I write, a debate is taking place over the ability of the police to make unannounced sweeps of housing projects where danger is a pervasive presence. The point is to disarm those who threaten and kill their brothers and sisters in alarming numbers. The people who live in these sites and who are striving with what can only be called heroism to protect their children welcome such police initiatives and can point to their concrete beneficial results. Mike Barnicle, a columnist for the *Boston Globe,* told the story of a thirty-one-year-old mother with three children, who called the police for months with stories of kids on her block "who were dealing daily in guns and drugs and creating such a climate of such fear that anyone interested in living normally found it an impossible task." She lined her walls and windows with mattresses to try to hide and perhaps to absorb bullets. When the police implemented a policy called Stop and Search, she and other mothers in the project rejoiced: Maybe, at long last, things would get better.

But, in Barnicle's words, "it ended almost as quickly as it began after lawyers and editorial writers came to the conclusion that it was a tremendous abridgement of the Constitution." So violence prospers, in part, because "simple items like a curfew" get dismissed as inherently coercive. Barnicle listed a few of the rights not currently

> accorded a young black mother and her three children: the right to sit on a stoop or at a playground. The right to walk to a store at any reasonable time . . . without the fear of getting caught in the cross fire. The right to spend a peaceful evening inside their own apartment. The right to stare out a window. The right of free association. The right to use a swing set whenever the whim strikes. The

right to complain publicly about gangsters in their midst. The right to be rid of crack and cocaine in the hallway and the vestibule. The right to life.

Kids with 9-millimeter guns—or larger—have their rights, and "a mother of three children has her mattresses in front of the window of her apartment."[26]

The social covenantee recognizes that market strategies are ill designed to speak directly to what concerns people the most in the worst inner-city neighborhoods. He or she would tell gun advocates and libertarians that, yes, murderers do kill people, but they use guns to do it. Surely you favor removing guns from the hands of dangerous people. Can you not assume that a fourteen-year-old drug-using dropout is dangerous, or potentially so? Would his freedom be unduly hampered if we made certain that he did not carry a gun into a school, a schoolyard, or a supermarket? The libertarian might respond that it is against the law for minors to carry loaded firearms. But the tough-minded advocate of a social covenant would parry, "Yes, I know that. But the fact of the matter is that children in America's inner cities are armed and dangerous, primarily to one another. Surely we can begin the process of disarming!"

Take a second case. To those prepared to excuse violent outrages on the grounds that looting, pillaging, burning, beating, and bashing people's heads in with bricks are expressions of rage at social injustice, the social covenant message is to call things by their real names. When I read headlines in certain so-called progressive journals in the aftermath of the 1992 riots in Los Angeles proclaiming L.A. UPRISING! or L.A. REBELLION, I felt real chagrin. A paternalistic attitude that refuses to consider all citizens as responsible is anathema to the democratic ethos. To excuse or even condone random violence—marked not by marches, organizing, issuing manifestos, and cobbling together a political program or vision, however rough-and-ready, but by the brutal destruction of persons and property—is to perpetrate a sickly fascination with violence, as if shedding blood were an inherently political act, and a radical one at that.

Such bewitchment with violence not only ill serves its victims, primarily those in the neighborhoods where the riots occurred, but perpetuates what political philosopher Hannah Arendt found to be one of the most pervasive and dangerous ideas (and she indicted the Left and Right alike for their enchantment with it at different times and in different places): that something good comes out of something evil, that authentic politics flows from the barrel of a gun, a knife blade, or a gasoline bomb. In the words of legal theorist Stephen Carter:

> We must never lose the capacity for judgment, especially the capacity to judge ourselves and our people. . . . Standards of morality matter no less than standards of excellence. There are black people who commit heinous crimes, and not all of them are driven by hunger and neglect. Not all of them turn to crime because they are victims of racist social policy. . . . We are not automatons. To understand all may indeed be to forgive all, but no civilization can survive when the capacity for understanding is allowed to supersede the capacity for judgment. Otherwise, at the end of the line lies a pile of garbage: Hitler wasn't evil, just insane.[27]

Government can be effective in lowering the homicide and terror rates in inner-city neighborhoods by helping to stitch community institutions back together. We do not need to abolish the Bill of Rights to accomplish this goal. But we do need, as a first step, to break through cynicism and anomie and to reverse the spiral of delegitimation. The democratic social covenant rests on the presumption that one's fellow citizens are people of goodwill who yearn for the opportunity to work together, rather than to continue to glare at one another across racial, class, and ideological divides. To accomplish this reversal, we must tend to the badly battered institutions of civil society I discussed at the outset.

An enormous task, yes, but worth our best efforts. As we enter the twenty-first century, we may learn, perhaps sooner than we would like, whether Lincoln's expression of the hope of American democracy was an epitaph or the harbinger of a brighter democratic future for America, and hence for the world. For if the American republic falters, it will be the crash heard 'round the world. Our many friends in other countries, especially in the young and fragile democracies, may tremble and perhaps fail without the ballast that America uniquely provides, given her power and her promise. That is the glorious burden of American democracy in the next century.

When I was asked by Jamie Swift, a broadcaster who was putting together a radio series on "The U.S.A. Today" for broadcast on CBC's *Ideas,* "What does it mean to you to be an American?" I stammered and mumbled for a moment before I got my bearings and responded:

It means that one can share a dream of political possibility, which is to say, a dream of democracy; it means that one can make one's voice heard; it means both individual accomplishment as well as a sense of responsibility; it means sharing the possibility of a brotherhood and sisterhood that is perhaps fractious—as all brotherhoods and sisterhoods are—and yet united in a spirit that's a spirit more of good than ill will; it means that one is marked by history but not totally burdened with it and defined by it; it means that one can expect some basic sense of fair play . . . will be recalled and called upon. I think Americans are committed to a rough-and-ready sense of fair play, and a kind of *social* egalitarianism, if you will, an egalitarianism of manners. I think that's the best I can do.

I will try to do better in the next chapter in which I home in on a politics of displacement, a politics that dislodges the concerns of the citizen and public life in favor of politicizing all features of who and what we are.

2

The Politics of Displacement

HAVE we democratic citizens become more fearful than hopeful? I suggested as much in the previous chapter, in which I surveyed the deepening anxiety, anger, resentment, and apathy that put democracies on trial. I also expressed my hearty dissent from a few ostensibly populist remedies for this collective condition. Let me remind you of a few of our most paralyzing collective fears: the next generation's way of life will not be better than that of previous generations; America's position in the world will falter; communities will continue to disintegrate; families will continue to collapse; the center simply will not hold. Fearful, we retreat or participate in the politics of resentment—finding somebody or some group to blame for all our ills: foreigners without, enemies within. If the great Roman republican citizen Cicero lamented that "we have lost the res publica," I bemoan the loss of something similar, the public citizen, and I embrace, as an alternative, a new social covenant in which we reach out once more to our fellow citizens from a stance of goodwill and work to defuse our discontents, so we might forge working alliances across various groups. Then and only then, I suggest, can we reclaim the great name *citizen*. For *citizen* is the name we give to our public identities and actions in a democratic society.

But wait, some readers will surely proclaim, do we not daily see frenetic activity, as people take to the streets and the airwaves demanding recognition for who and what they are? Is there not already a great deal of what I described in chapter 1 as active participation—lobbying, meeting, marching, debating? Is this not citizenship of the robust sort?

I must demur and hope that I will be successful, in what follows, in explaining the distinction between what I tag the *politics of displacement* and authentic democratic possibilities. Roughly put, the politics of displacement involves two trajectories. In the first, everything private—from one's sexual practices to blaming one's parents for one's lack of "self-esteem"— becomes grist for the public mill. In the second, everything public—from the grounds on which politicians are judged to health policies to gun regulations—is privatized and played out in a psychodrama on a grand scale, that is, we fret as much about a politician's sexual life as about his foreign policy; or we favor insured health care only if it pays for our own guaranteed comfort, described as medical needs or even aesthetic wants, and oppose it if it does not; or we see in firearm regulation only an assault, no doubt limited and imperfect, on our identity as gun-toting vigilantes, rather than as a way to try to control slaughter in our streets without eroding the rights of hunters and others.

The complete collapse of a distinction between public and private is anathema to democratic thinking, which holds that the differences between public and private identities, commitments, and activities are of vital importance. Historically, it has been the antidemocrats who have insisted that political life must be cut from one piece of cloth; they have demanded overweening and unified loyalty to the monarch or the state, unclouded by other passions, commitments, and interests. Something similar is going on as politics gets displaced in the ways I will reveal, beginning with a reminder of what democrats are talking about when they evoke the terms *public* and *private*.

PUBLIC AND PRIVATE

"Public" and "private" are terms of ordinary discourse, always defined and understood in relation to each other. One definition of *private* is "not open to the public," and the common definition of public is "of or pertaining to the whole, done or made in behalf of the community as a whole." In part, these contrasts derive from the Latin word for public, *pubes,* which refers to the age of maturity, when signs of puberty begin to appear; then and only then does the child enter, or become qualified for, public things. Similarly, *publicus* is that which belongs to, or pertains to, "the public," the people. But there is another meaning of public: open to scrutiny; and of private: what is not subjected to the persistent gaze of publicity. This barrier to full revelation is necessary, or so defenders of constitutional democracy have long insisted, to preserve the possibility of different sorts of relationships—both the mother *and* the citizen, the friend *and* the official, and so on.

Minimally, a *political* perspective requires us to differentiate the activity we call "politics" from other activities and relationships. If all conceptual boundaries are blurred and all distinctions between public and private eliminated, no politics can exist, by definition. By *politics,* I refer to that which is, in principle, held in common and what is, in principle, open to public scrutiny and judgment. If I am correct that politics of displacement is a growing phenomenon, operating on the level of elite opinion and popular culture alike, especially in America, it bears deep implications for how we will think about and conduct politics in the years ahead. In our boredom and our despair, we take to the airwaves and the streets to proclaim the awful and ugly truth about a spouse, a friend, a lover, a parent, a child, or a despised enemy or group. And this ugly phenomenon, this eruption of *publicity* and the substitute of publicity for that which is authentically either private or public, is now America's leading growth industry.

A politics of displacement is a dynamic that connects and interweaves public and private imperatives in a way that is dangerous to the integrity of both. It is more likely for a politics of displacement to take hold when certain conditions prevail. First, established public and private, secular and religious institutions and rules are in flux, and people have a sense that the center does not hold. Second, there are no clearly established public institutions to focus dissent and concern. Third, and finally, private values, exigencies, and identities come to take precedence in all things, including public involvement as a citizen.[1]

This, clearly, is the world we are now in. But note that *private* here does not refer to our need to preserve certain

THE POLITICS OF DISPLACEMENT

relationships and institutions but rather to that diminished universe of one: me and my fleeting angers, resentments, sentiments, and impulses. A recent important study, based on group discussions with involved citizens, found that people depend on "little-noticed meeting places—places of worship, libraries, community halls—where they can interact with others, offer their own thinking and become committed to, and sometimes engaged in, the solution [to a political question or problem]. These places are becoming fewer, the researchers said."[2] The fewer such civic sites, the more likely is a politics of displacement.

A displaced politics features a world of triumphalist I's, "a population of monads . . . , simple, irreducible entities, each defined by a unique point of view," in the words of political theorist Sheldon Wolin.[3] To the extent that there is a "we" in this world of I's, it is that of the discrete group with whom the I identifies. For example, in current debates over multiculturalism, some argue that if one is an African American, one must "think black" and identify exclusively with one's racial group or designation. Similarly, a white person "thinks white" and cannot do otherwise. For persons thus identified, the category of "citizen" is a matter of indifference at best, contempt at worst. Increasingly, we come to see ourselves exclusively along racial or gender or sexual-preference lines. If this is who I am, why should I care about the citizen? That is for dupes who actually believed their high school civics teacher.

To the extent that a politics of displacement pertains, all is defined as "political" and watered down to the lowest common denominator. Thus, as I indicated in the first chapter, everything I "want" gets defined politically as a "right." Thus, for example, my desire, now a right, to have easy access to a pornography channel on cable television is conflated with my right to be safe from arrest or torture for my political views. Civil rights are trivialized in this process. Political ideals and private desires are blurred or collapsed. By extension, of course, there is no such thing as an authentically private sphere. Intimate life is pervaded with politics; private identity becomes a recommendation for, or authentication of, one's political stance. It follows that my rage quotient goes through the roof in political contestation, because to argue against my subjective pronouncements is also to unhinge my private identity. This is muddled thinking, of course, but it seems to be where we are—to our own peril and that of our civic descendants.

Take, for example, the 1970s feminist slogan "The personal is political." On the one hand, this was an exciting and transformative move, compelling men and women to attend to the undeniable fact that certain political interests were often hidden behind a gloss of professed concern for the sanctity of the private realm. Feminists argued that political and ethical values were often trivialized by being privatized, as a whole range of questions regarding women, children, and families was sealed off as irrelevant to political discussion and debate. Children's health, for example, was the private concern of parents, especially mothers. But what if there is asbestos in the insulation of the local school building, and it is well known that asbestos causes health problems? Surely, here, the threat to health is a public one, involving all children who attend that school and their families. To politicize and to challenge the notion of separate spheres—the male public world and the female private world—in this way was a vital and important civic possibility. Feminists who were committed to ideals of civility and civic culture recognized that there are many ways to carve up the universe of debate in social and political life.

But from the beginning, there were problems embedded in the assertion that the personal is political *tout court*. In its give-no-quarter form in radical feminist argument, any distinction between the personal and political was disdained. Note that the claim was not that the personal and political are interrelated in ways previously hidden by male-dominated political ideology and practice, or that the personal and political might be analogous to each other along certain axes of power and privilege. Rather, there was a collapse of one into the other: The personal *is* political. Nothing personal was exempt from political definition, direction, and manipulation—not sexual intimacy, not love, not parenting. The total collapse of public and private as central distinctions in an enduring democratic drama followed, at least in theory. The private sphere fell under a thoroughgoing politicized definition. Everything was grist for a voracious publicity mill; nothing was exempt, there was nowhere to hide. This situation got nasty fast. For example, I have been involved in these debates long enough to recall the time when women who married and bore children became the target of all sorts of polemical assaults in feminist argumentation. They were "collabos," women who collaborated with the male "enemy," women who had been turned into "mutilated, muted, moronized . . . docile tokens mouthing male texts"—not a generous image, to say the least, but one made possible by defining male-female relationships as *essentially* those of a victimizer to a victim.[4]

But more serious than the problem of rhetorical excess is the one that puts democracy continuously on trial: If there are no distinctions between public and private, personal and political, it follows that there can be no differentiated activity or set of institutions that are genuinely political, the purview of citizens and the bases of order, legitimacy, and purpose in a democratic community. As columnist and writer Christopher Hitchens, himself a person of the Left, wrote: "I remember feeling an uneasy premonition when, in the period of defeat and demoralization that followed the 1960s, it was decided that the left could be revived with the assertion that 'the personal is political.' The consequences of that rather dubious claim are now all around us, except that personality has deposed politics altogether."[5] If genuine politics ceases to exist, what rushes in to take its place is pervasive force, coercion, and manipulation: power of the crassest sort suffusing the entire social landscape, from its lowest to its loftiest points. If you live in a world of pervasive fear and anxiety, a world this sort of rhetoric helps to construct, you become ripe—or the story of Western political thought warns us—for antidemocratic solutions. If the problem is totalistic, so must the solution be. This goes against the grain of the democratic temperament, one always aware that no single perspective, no single political platform or slogan, can speak the whole truth about our situation.

There are few alternatives in such a world: One is either victim or victimizer, oppressed or oppressor, abject or triumphant. Politics as a particular sphere of human activity disappears in this yearning for a totalistic solution to all human woes, this world of refined and competing resentments. The possibility that certain vital relationships are possible *only* because they take place beyond the full glare of public scrutiny and preserve others against scrutiny (snooping by roaming Nosy Parkers, as my British friends call them) is simply forsworn. Do I exaggerate? Perhaps. But let us take a closer look. I hope to convince you that my concerns and criticisms are warranted from a democratic point of view. We have long been familiar with the terrible invasion of private life and speech characteristic of twentieth-century totalitarian societies. People in such situations learn to censor themselves or, growing careless, may find that conversation around a kitchen table or in the bedroom with one's spouse becomes the public property of the police or, worse, of the entire society.

In a 1984 interview with Philip Roth, the Czech novelist Milan Kundera noted a "magic border" between "intimate life and public life . . . that can't be crossed with impunity," for any "man who was the same in both public and intimate life would be a monster." Says Kundera:

> He would be without spontaneity in his private life and without responsibility in his public life. For example, privately to you I can say of a friend who's done something stupid, that he's an idiot, that his ears ought to be cut off, that he should be hung upside down and a mouse stuffed in his mouth. But if the same statement were broadcast over the radio spoken in a serious tone—and we all prefer to make such jokes in a serious tone—it would be indefensible.[6]

Kundera went on to recall the tragedy of a friend, a writer named Jan Prochazka, whose intimate "kitchen table" talks were recorded by the state police in pre-1989 Czechoslo-vakia and assembled into a "program" that was broadcast on state radio: "He finds himself in a state of complete humilia-tion: the secret eye observes him even when he kisses his wife in the bedroom or stands in front of the toilet bowl. Such a man can only die"—as Prochazka did, humiliated by his ordeal. According to Kundera, *intimate life*—a creation of European civilization "during the last 400 years," understood as "one's personal secret, as something valuable, inviolable, the basis of one's originality"—is now in jeopardy everywhere, not just in statist societies with a secret police apparatus.

Are his fears well placed? Consider two examples drawn from contemporary American society, both of which flow from the collapse of the personal into the political and therefore exemplify the politics of displacement. Of course, there are no precise parallels in a democratic society to the terror Kundera so poignantly described. But we have our own "soft" versions of an utter disregard for public and private distinctions.

THE IDEOLOGY OF
WOMEN'S VICTIMIZATION

For my first example, let me zero in on battered women and take up various solutions to the problem proposed by some analysts and activists that display and deepen a politics of dis-placement, turning, as they do, on the erosion of any public-private distinction. The first assertion usually made, one that all fair-minded persons will surely endorse, is that domestic violence is not just a private affair; we must all be concerned when a fellow citizen is assaulted, degraded, and denied dignity. But if you are working from a perspective that erodes *any* distinction between public and private and you find this assertion nothing more than bourgeois hypocrisy, your proposed solutions start to take on many features of antidemocratic totalism.

The standard totalist case works like this: We must, as part of an interim strategy, expand the arrest powers of the police and promote the jurisprudential conviction that women are a special legal category requiring unique protection.[7] Precious little attention is paid to the fact that enhancing police and juridical prerogatives to intervene may lead to the abuse of society's least powerful, such as poor blacks and Hispanics, should they be deemed the most menacing members of a generic male threat. When this potential danger is acknowledged, it is usually seen as a chance worth taking. Mandated counseling, even behavioral conditioning of violent or "potentially violent" men, coupled with compulsory punishment and no appeal, are common parts of the panoply of interim proposals that have been made; the potential abuses inherent in extending the therapeutic powers of the state as part of its policing function are commonly ignored. Indeed, the history of the so-called social hygiene movements of the late-nineteenth and early-twentieth centuries in the United States and Canada tells us as much. In those movements, "women's sexuality" was policed and restricted to certain standards of class and ethnicity. The dangerous impulsive threat of black men, the crafty wiles of Italian seducers, and the opium-inflamed manipulations of Chinese "white slavers" fed the moral panic and calls for, among other things, restrictions on immigration and harsh treatment of black men—who were accused of such infractions as "reckless eyeballing."

These programs and their contemporary analogues rely heavily on the state's policing powers, which, in other contexts, are trounced as being part of the patriarchal order. But that is only the beginning in totalist scenarios that locate the *solution* to the problem of violence once and for all in a "total restructuring of society that is feminist, antiracist, and socialist," in the words of one advocate.[8] It is unclear whether such a society would be democratic or whether, indeed, there would be any politics worthy of the name at all. Remember the Marxist dream that one glorious day politics will come to an end, absorbed into administration in the classless society. Presumably in this radical feminist version of an ideal future, some sort of powerful state must be on hand to plan everything and to redistribute, given the commitment to socialism, but this is not spelled out.

Most important, in this new society as imagined by radical activist and writer Susan Schechter,

> family life would be open for *community scrutiny* because the family would be part of and accountable to the community. Community-based institutions could hear complaints and dispense justice, and community networks could hold individuals accountable for their behavior and offer protection to women. If a *false separation* did not exist between the family and the community, women might lose their sense of isolation and gain a sense of entitlement to a violence-free life.[9]

But what about the repressive potential of the all-powerful "community institutions" and the policing state here envisaged? The author of this plan for eviscerating any public-private distinction goes no further in specifying how this robust communitarian world—a future perfect gemeinschaft—is to be generated out of what she portrays as our current battlefield.

Because Schechter assumes that "total restructuring" will produce a moral consensus, all dissidents having been banished, silenced, punished, or reeducated, she skirts problems of coercion and control that are otherwise implicit in her scheme for hearing complaints and dispensing justice with no provisions for the accused to be defended or his accusers cross-examined, and certainly no presumption of innocence until proven guilty. With every aspect of life opened up for inspection and, in her words, scrutiny, Schechter prescribes a world that democrats must find singularly unattractive.[10]

Even in old-fashioned traditional communities of the sort I grew up in, a rural Colorado village of 185, there was room for backsliders, town drunks, loners, dreamers, and harmless eccentrics. Why do these prophets of totally restructured worlds "beyond compromise" not tell us what will happen to such folks in their brave new societies? Not every social misfit is a violent abuser. In the society of scrutiny, total accountability, and instant justice, the social space for difference, dissent, refusal, and indifference is squeezed out. This is where matters stand unless or until advocates who share this theoretical orientation tell us how the future community of scrutiny will preserve any freedom worthy of the name. I doubt that those who make such proposals have really considered the implications of their arguments for democratic civil life. For example, con-

tained within the paean to intrusive communities in a reconstructed future is the unequivocal claim that "who women
choose as emotional and sexual partners cannot be open for
public scrutiny"—an embrace of the public-private distinction
and the possibility for concealment wholly at odds with the
plans for a society in which "family life will be open to community scrutiny."[11]

There seem to be a few loose threads dangling here. A
more democratic way of tending to these matters is to begin
by giving individuals wide berth in ordering their private lives
as they see fit. The public's interest becomes legitimate when
there is a pattern of physical harm that is persistent, not hap-
hazard—when one family member is beaten or bruised or
injured by another. No democratic society can permit such
assaults to persist. We have devised ways—imperfect, to be
sure—of dealing with such situations that preserve our simulta-
neous commitment to protection for those who are harmed
and due process for those who are accused. What seems to be
lacking in too many cases is rigorous enforcement of extant
statutes and bringing the full force of the law to bear against
violent offenders. In part through the efforts of feminist orga-
nizers, the issue of battered women is now widely accepted as
a public, not merely a private, concern. This is as it should be,
but it is quite different from arguing that everything that goes
on inside a family ought to be subject to public scrutiny.

Such conjecture leads to another related concern: the
notion that women are society's prototypical victims. There
are, of course, real victims in the world, and among their number are all too many women. But an ideology of victimhood
diverts attention from concrete and specific instances of female

victimization in favor of pushing a relentless worldview struc-tured around the victim-victimizer dichotomy. The aim is to promote what can only be called moral panic, as women are routinely portrayed as helpless and demeaned. Note that the language of victimization describes women in passive terms. Jettisoning all the complexities of real victimization, it recasts women as helpless prey to male lust and assault. According to this, *all* women are assaulted, though some may not yet recog-nize it; all are harmed, one way or another. The ideology of victimization fuels women's fear and, paradoxically, disem-powers them; it does not enable them to see themselves as citizens with both rights and responsibilities.

Eight years ago, I researched the issue of women as vic-tims of crime. I learned that, on the best available evidence, the assertion that women are the *principal* victims of violent crime is false: The most vulnerable body to inhabit in America today, as it was when I conducted my research, is that of a young black male. As well, on the best available evidence, vio-lence against women is *not* on a precipitous upsurge com-pared with other crimes. Yet popular perception, fueled by the victimization narrative, holds otherwise. As a result, women are more likely to *think* of themselves as crime victims: They have assumed an ideology of victimization that is startlingly out of proportion to the actual threat. The perception of "women as victims" goes beyond a deeply rooted belief that violence against women is skyrocketing; it holds that women are special targets of crime in general and of violent crime in particular. Yet the figures on this score have been remarkably consistent over the past decade: Most perpetrators of violent crimes are young males; most victims of violent crimes are males similar in age and race to the perpetrators. And, as I already indicated, African American youths are the most threatened of all.

The fear-of-crime syndrome has a debilitating effect on behavior, as women internalize a distorted perception of themselves. For example, in 1991, half of the 250 American movies made for television depicted women undergoing abuse of one kind or another. This could give television viewers the impression that women have a 50 percent chance each week of being victims of a violent crime. Often such trashy programs are given a feminist gloss, but by portraying women in peril in the home, the workplace, and the street, they ill serve women or any feminism worthy of the name. Women are shown either as trembling wrecks or as fierce avengers with scant regard for what is usually called due process.

IDENTITY POLITICS: GAY LIBERATION OR CIVIC EQUALITY?

My second example of the politics of displacement is drawn from the intense arena of so-called identity politics, which I will cover in greater detail in chapter 3 when I discuss democratic education and the politics of difference. But it is important to introduce the theme here under the rubric of the politics of displacement. Remember that a central characteristic of the politics of displacement is that private identity takes precedence over public ends or purposes; indeed, one's private identity becomes who and what one is *in public,* and public life is about confirming that identity. The citizen gives way before the aggrieved member of a self-defined or contained group. Because the group is aggrieved—the word of choice in most polemics is *enraged*—the civility inherent in those rule-governed activities that allow a pluralist society to persist falters. This assault on civility flows from an embrace of what might be called a politicized ontology—that is, persons are to be judged not by what they do or say but by what they *are*. What you are is what your racial or sexual identity dictates. Your identity becomes the sole ground of politics, the sole determinant of political good and evil. Those who disagree with my "politics," then, are the enemies of my identity.

For my example of identity politics, I turn to the important controversies generated by the gay liberation movement. Gay liberation, in its displaced version, stands in contrast to an equal rights agenda, including a demand for dignity and recognition based on an inclusive democratic strategy. I have participated in this latter effort myself, chairing a task force that established the Committee on the Status of Lesbians and Gays for the American Political Science Association. The task force's statement of principles emphasized collegiality and dignity and the insistence that anyone hired to join an academic department should be invited to participate fully in the life of that department, without regard to sexual orientation. Bad behavior is bad behavior, no matter who commits it, and only behavior, not identity, should be criticized. "Hitting on" students is gauche and unacceptable, whether the lech in question is gay or straight.

But mark this: From the beginning of the movement for gay liberation, there was tension in the claim that gays, labeled an "oppressed class" by radical theorists, were forced to call on the very society that was oppressing them not only to protect their rights but to legitimate what became known as a "homosexual ethos" or a "gay lifestyle." The argument that gays are oppressed, then, results in two different claims: either that society has no business scrutinizing the private sexual preferences of anybody, including gays; or that government *must* intrude in the area of private identity because gays, like women, require a unique sort of public protection and "validation," in today's lexicon.[12] The politics of democratic civility and equity holds that *all* citizens, including gays, have a right, as individuals, to be protected from intrusion or harassment and to be free from discrimination in such areas as employment and housing. They also have a right to create their own forms of "public space" within which to express and to reveal their particular concerns and to argue in behalf of policies they support. This I take as a given when a public-private distinction of a certain sort is cherished and upheld. This distinction is an ongoing imperative in a democratic constitutional system; ignoring or violating it is not only an illegality but an assault on the constitutive political ethic of a democratic society.

But no one has a *civil* right, as a gay, a disciple of an exotic religion, or a political dissident, to full public sanction of his or her activities, values, beliefs, or habits. To be publicly legitimated, or "validated," in one's activities, beliefs, or habits may be a political aim—indeed, it is the overriding aim of the politics of displacement—but it is hardly a civil right. Paradoxically, in his quest to attain sanction for the *full* range of who he is, the cross-dresser or sadomasochist, the variations are nigh endless, puts his life on full display. He opens himself up to *publicity* in ways that others are bound to find quite uncivil, in part because a certain barrier—the political philosopher Hannah Arendt would have called it the boundary of shame—is harshly breached.

I readily concede that "shame" has few defenders as we near the end of the twentieth century in the West. But I hope you will hear me out. If, as I have argued, and many of my betters before me, notably Tocqueville, have insisted, democracy is about not only constitutions, rules, public accountability, and deliberation but also everyday life, habits, and dispositions, then it makes some sense to think about shame and shamelessness. Shame—or its felt experience as it surrounds our body's functions, passions, and desires—requires veils of civility that conceal some activities and aspects of ourselves even as we boldly and routinely display and reveal others when we take part in public activities for all to see. When one's intimate life is put on display on television or the streets or in other public spaces, one not only invites but actively seeks the exploitation of one's body to a variety of ends not fully under one's control. For one has then withdrawn the body's intimacy from interpersonal relations and exposed it to an unknown audience. Thus one may become an occasion for scandal or abuse or even violence toward others through one's relentless self-exposure. Flaunting one's most intimate self, making a public thing of oneself, is central to the politics of displacement, no matter who undertakes it—gay or straight; arguing for a position, winning approval, or inviting dissent as a citizen is something quite different.

Shame is central to safeguarding the freedom of the body: small wonder, then, that so many philosophers, theologians, and political theorists have found in shame, or the need for privacy and concealment, a vital and powerful feature of our human condition that we would overturn at our peril. This is not to embrace duplicity and disguise; rather, it means holding on to the concealment necessary for a rich personal life and human dignity. We emerge from our very particular, private sites into the exposure of a public existence where we can come to know and thus work to attain what is at once self-revelatory and central to human solidarity and fellowship—what is in common. There have been times in our century—terrible times—when this notion has come home to people in the most brutal way. Dietrich Bonhoeffer, the great German theologian and martyr to the anti-Nazi cause, wrote that shame is not "good in itself" and that to argue that way is "moralistic, puritanical, totally unbiblical." Rather, shame gives "reluctant witness to its own fallen state." From this division, this recognition of our incompleteness, the human being "does not show himself in its nakedness."[13] Indeed, we can go public only from a stance of rectitude that permits us to respect others as we cannot if we are driven by a longing for the innocence of the Garden, a yearning to restore a lost unity. Hence Bonhoeffer's condemnation of the ideologue, the one who sees himself justified in his own idea, through his very shamelessness. The ideologue looks into the mirror of the self and declares it good: he is a child of light; the others are the minions of darkness. We breach the boundary of shame at our risk, Bonhoeffer suggests, for what gets unleashed may in the end destroy much more than it saves or preserves.

How does all this bear on our current politics of displacement? The thread of the arguments I am tying together begins with the recognition that in Western democracies governed by notions of rights and the rule of law, the politically and culturally different have traditionally embraced certain principles of civility as their best and most enduring guarantee that government will not try to coerce them to concur with, or conform to, the majority. If I go about my business respectful of the fact that you, too, must go about yours, we need not share or even understand each other's beliefs, rituals, and values completely. But we do understand that we share a civil world—that we are, for better or for worse, "in it together."

Militant liberationists, in contrast to civil-society activists, seek official, mandated protection and approval of their private identities and behavior. These claims against society require public remedies. To this end, some go so far as to endorse wrenching disclosures and invasions of the privacy of others, called "outing"—whereby those who prefer not to go public with their homosexual orientation are forced "into the open" by others who publish their names in newspapers, post their pictures on telephone posts, or broadcast their names at rallies. Such an activity may well have the practical result of strengthening the ethos of a society of scrutiny: Nothing is exempt, if not from one's "enemies," then, ironically, even tragically, from one's ostensible friends and allies. As a result, the demand for public validation of sexual preferences, by ignoring the distinction between the personal and the political, threatens to erode authentic civil rights, including the right to privacy. Recently, important homosexual writers and analysts have opened up this debate and invited all of us, whatever our sexual orientation, to participate.[14]

What follows from these brave forays into civil society is often lively disputation from those who do not share one's orientation and heated denunciation from the totalists who do. This should not surprise us. For those who push a strong version of identity politics, any politics that does not revolve around their identities is of no interest to them. There is no broader identification with a common good beyond that of the group of which one is a member. Hence the argument made during the Vietnam War by an identity-politics activist that gays "do not get validated by our participation in anti-war marches" becomes understandable because in those marches one made common cause with other citizens who found the war abhorrent. If politics is reducible to the "eruption of radical feelings," something as seemingly "ordinary" as protest against an unjust war lacks radical panache.[15] Personal authenticity becomes the test of political credibility. One can cure one's personal ills only through political rebellion based on sexual identity. The demands that issue from such a politics of displacement go far beyond the quest for civic freedom and for what Greek democrats called *isonomia,* or equality: Nothing less than personal happiness and sexual gratification are claimed as *political* rights. And one cannot even reach the stage of *disagreement.* Philosopher James L. Nash aired his frustration on this score, recounting a failed attempt at a "gay/straight dialogue":

> In one of the first programs, I began to stake out what I hoped would be common ground, a "staging area" for further exploration, by asking if the other panelists accepted the value of fidelity in sexual intimacy, no matter what the orientation of partners. My lesbian conversation partner declared that she regarded sexual fidelity as

an alien value which heterosexuals, especially male heterosexuals, were unjustly and oppressively seeking to
impose on her. Moreover, she argued that by holding
sexual promiscuity to be somehow morally inferior to
fidelity, I was adopting a position which was tantamount
to homophobia. Naturally I resisted her presupposition
that gay people are more promiscuous than straight folk,
and that therefore my position entailed an antigay prejudice. She disagreed. End of conversation.[16]

Both homosexuals and heterosexuals have altogether too
many "end of conversation" weapons in our armamentaria
today. The victim is civic life in the here and now and, over
time, a polity worthy of being called democratic.

THE DEMOCRATIC IDEAL

The demand upon activists themselves is extreme, for every
aspect of their lives must serve as a political statement. There
is no surcease, no way to say, "To hell with it, I'm going fishing. I'll be a militant again in two weeks." There is good reason for the democrat to be queasy about too much resolute
militancy. Identity absolutism lends itself to expressivist politics, the celebration of feelings or private authenticity as an
alternative to public debate and political judgment. Where is
the check on overpersonalization? There is none. It is perhaps useful at this juncture to remind those who eschew a
public-private distinction that the world is much wider,
deeper, and more mysterious than a wholesale mapping of

the subjective self onto that world suggests. It is a world with saving graces, a world, one hopes of veils as well as mirrors, a world filled with all sorts of people with ingrained predispositions that may not be trimmed precisely to fit the pattern we dictate. When utopians of any stripe assault the idea of political standing in and through an ideal of the citizen, they promote the diminution of democratic politics in favor of a fantasy of either a wholly transparent community in which all that divides us has been eliminated or one in which our divisions are "beyond compromise." At the height of the 1960s civil rights movement in America, Martin Luther King, Jr., declared that he and his fellow citizen-protesters were not asking their opponents to love them; rather, "We're just asking you to get off our backs."

King's dream of a new democratic community, a new social covenant, drew upon old democratic ideas forged on the anvil of his rock-bottom Christian faith. In the pragmatic yet idealistic world of practical politics that King endorsed, blacks and whites, men and women, the poor and the privileged, come together around a set of concrete concerns. Temporary alliances are formed, though the assumption is never that things will automatically divide by a racial or any other identity. For practical politics to thrive, there must be a way for people who differ in important respects to come together. This distinction between public and private life grows from a recognition that people's self-interests or personal travail may lead them to public action, but the best principles of action in public are not reducible to merely private matters. In public we learn to work with people with whom we disagree sharply and with whom we would not care to live in a situation of intimacy. But we can be citizens together; we can come to know a good in common that we cannot know alone.

When I was in graduate school in the late 1960s, it was in vogue to mock the warnings of political philosopher Isaiah Berlin about the dangers inherent in many visions of "positive liberty," turning as they did on naive views of a perfectible human nature and a utopian projection of a political solution to every human frailty and ill. Those who embraced positive liberty believed that the only politics worthy of the name must engage in a massive rearrangement of human societies to attain an abstract goal like justice or happiness on earth. Berlin was accused of being a "liberal sellout," a fainthearted compromiser, because he found such pictures of a perfect future reality implausible.[17] But compromise is not a mediocre way to do politics; it is an adventure, the *only* way to do democratic politics. It lacks the seduction of revolutionary violence, whether rhetorical or enacted. It does not stir the blood in the way a "nonnegotiable demand" does. It is not Me demanding primacy for Myself. But it presages a livable future.

I am reminded of a conversation I had in Prague in the summer of 1990 with a former dissident who found himself elected to Parliament in the aftermath of the remarkable events of November 1989. He said to me, "We've got a real problem here because we are not habituated to democracy. We have had democratic moments in our past, but we don't have well-formed democratic dispositions. It will be difficult to build these up. It will take time. After all, the democratic ideal is a very difficult ideal."

I asked him what the democratic ideal meant, and he responded: "It is difficult, especially for people who have lived

in a system of totalistic politics, because it embeds at its heart
the ideal of compromise. In a democracy, compromise is not a
terrible thing. It is necessary; it lies at the heart of things
because you have to accept that people are going to have different views, especially on the most volatile matters and the
most important issues." His words struck me then and do so
now because Western democracies are not doing a good job of
nurturing those democratic dispositions that encourage people
to accept that they can't always get what they want and that
some of what they seek in politics cannot be found there.

In any democratic polity, there are choices to be made
that involve both gains and losses. Berlin reminds us that a
"sharp division between public and private life, or politics and
morality, never works well. Too many territories have been
claimed by both." But to collapse public and private altogether
is an even worse prospect, for, according to Berlin, "the best
that one can do is to try to promote some kind of equilibrium,
necessarily unstable, between the different operations of different groups of human beings—at the very least to prevent
them from attempting to exterminate one another and, so far
as possible, to prevent them from hurting each other—and to
promote the maximum practicable degree of sympathy and
understanding, never likely to be complete between them."[18]
This is a plea for practical politics within a democratic polity
characterized by civility and open to the possibility of achiev-
ing working majorities, provisional commonalities, and, no
doubt, ephemeral moments of civic virtue.

To survive, a richly complex private sphere requires freedom from an all-encompassing public imperative. But to flourish, the public world itself must nurture and sustain a set of

ethical imperatives, including a commitment to preserve, protect, and defend human beings in their capacities as private
individuals and public citizens engaged in the practical activity
of democratic life. This ideal keeps alive a fruitful if, at times,
frustrating tension between diverse spheres and competing
ideals and purposes. There is always the danger that an overly
strong and overweening polity will swamp the individual, as
well as the danger that life in a polity confronted with a continuing crisis, the politics of displacement, may decivilize both
those who oppose it and those who promote it.

3

The Politics of Difference

THE question of unity and diversity has been posed from the beginning of political thought in the West. The American Founders were well aware of the vexations attendant upon the creation of a new political body. They worked with, and against, metaphors that had once served as the symbolic vehicles of political incorporation. As men of the Enlightenment, they rejected images of the body politic that had dominated medieval and early-modern political thinking. For Jefferson, Madison, and others, political theories of "the King's two bodies"—John of Salisbury's twelfth-century vision in *Politicraticus* of a body politic with the prince as the head and animating force—were too strongly corporatist, predemocratic, and explicitly Christian to serve the *novus ordo seclorum*.[1] But they were haunted nonetheless by Hebrew and Christian metaphors of a covenanted polity: The body is one but has many members.

Indeed, one might argue that it is only incorporation within a single body that makes meaningful diversity possible.

Our differences must be recognized if they are to exist substantively. As political philosopher Charles Taylor noted, "my discovering my own identity doesn't mean that I work it out in isolation, but that I negotiate it through dialogue, partly overt, partly internal, with others. . . . My own identity crucially depends on my dialogical relations with others."[2] In other words, we cannot be different all by ourselves. The great challenge for the Founders was to form a political body that brought people together and created a "we," but also enabled people to remain separate and to recognize and respect one another's differences. Modern democrats face the same challenge.

I indicated in chapter 2 that one version of our current discontents—the politics of displacement—tries to solve this problem by smashing it to bits. Rather than negotiating the complexity of public and private identities, those who adopt this view disdain and displace any distinction between the citizen and whatever else a person may be—male or female, heterosexual or homosexual, black or white. One seeks full public recognition as a person with a handicap or a particular sexual orientation, or membership in an ethnic or racial group, and that exhausts one's public concerns. Marks of difference, once they gain public recognition in this form, translate all too easily into group triumphalism as the story grows that the public world is a world of many I's who form a we only with others exactly like themselves. No recognition of commonality is forthcoming. We are stuck in what the philosopher calls a world of "incommensurability," a world in which we literally cannot understand one another.

Democrats historically would have found this notion

peculiar at best, anathema at worst. Democrats today are troubled by such developments. We recognize in the rush for recognition of difference a powerful, and legitimate, modern concern. Some forms of equal recognition surely not only are possible in a democracy but form its very lifeblood. The question is, What sort of recognition? Recognition of what? For what? To claim "I am different, you must recognize me and honor my difference" tells me nothing that is civically interesting. Should I honor or recognize someone simply because she is female or proclaims a particular version of her sexual identity? This would make little sense. I may disagree profoundly with her about everything I find important—from what American policy ought to be in the war in the Balkans, to what needs to be done to stem the tide of deterioration and despair in America's inner cities, to whether violence on television is a serious concern or just an easy target for riled and worried parents and educators.

My recognition of her difference, by which I mean my preparedness to engage her as an interlocutor *given* our differences on the things that count politically—including equality, justice, freedom, fairness, authority, and power—turns on the fact that I share something with her: She is in the world with me; she, too, is a citizen. We both, it is hoped, operate from a stance of goodwill and an acceptance of the backdrop of democratic constitutional guarantees, as well as democratic habits and dispositions. We are both committed to rough-and-ready parity, an energetic desire to forge at least provisional agreements on highly controversial issues or to remain committed to the centrality of dialogue and debate to our shared way of life if we cannot resolve our differences. If I am her enemy because I am white or heterosexual or a mother or an academic, or she is mine because she is none of these things, our only option is to "go to war"—to silence, reproach, even wipe out each other. One makes war with enemies; one does politics—democratic politics—with opponents.

DIFFERENCE AND INEQUALITY

I will turn later to how we come to know something "in common," to accept that we share a heritage, although we share it imperfectly and unevenly. But, first, let me say a bit more about the current politics of difference. At one point not so long ago, it was the liberal position that an emphasis on the ways people differed sanctioned inequality and that our "sameness" alone secured an egalitarian, democratic regime: If you prick me, do I not bleed? After all, was it not hierarchical, inegalitarian, conservative thinkers who insisted that natural differences must translate into social and political inequalities? American society is, perhaps, unique among nations in that, from the first, equality ("all men are created equal") has been one of the touchstones of its national identity and political culture. Need I acknowledge that slaves and women were omitted from the formal definition and struggled mightily for inclusion? But the general principle named both a partial and imperfect reality and a continuing aspiration.

For many conservatives, an extension of equality beyond legal recognition—and even that might be going too far—was balderdash because it was obvious to them that people were different from one another, indeed, unequal by nature. Such persons equated equality with sameness and inequality with difference. Because it is clear that human beings differ, they insisted, society must reflect those differences. Furthermore, they contended, we will invariably wind up with widespread social inequality because people are not the same; inequality is lodged in nature. It follows that attempts to alter institutions to eliminate or reduce inequality will require nasty social surgery, because we must then eliminate human differences them-selves. It seems best, according to this conservative argument, to allow natural differences—seen as inequalities—to work themselves out, even if the result is a stratified, inegalitarian society in the social and economic sense even as we remain equal only before the law.

Those who opposed this view, usually persons from the political Left or centrist liberals, insisted that it strained credulity to believe that all those who were well placed had fully earned it and that their power and privilege simply flowed from their being different—unequal—from the rest of us. Alas, the radical egalitarian response often got as tenden-tious as that of its ideological opposite. Rather than challenge the equation of equality with sameness, many critics implicitly embraced the idea: The more we were the same, the better. So they extolled a fuzzy or utopian notion of a world in which people were as indistinguishable from one another as happy peas in the egalitarian pod. Arguments defending the necessity to assess the disparate value or merit of diverse human capaci-ties, abilities, and achievements vanished like the early morn-ing dew in the sunlight's steady glare. I clearly remember the heated denunciations of "elitism" from my college compatriots in the 1960s whenever evaluations of merit and accomplishment were defended. Some argued that standards themselves are somehow inherently antidemocratic. The same argument is even more vehemently pressed today.

This vision of a bland equality of sameness was promoted by many calling themselves egalitarians, some of whom were indebted to Marxism. The American writer Kurt Vonnegut satirized it in his short story "Harrison Bergeron," which appears in a collection called *Welcome to the Monkey House:*

> The year was 2081 and everybody was finally equal. They weren't only equal before God and the law. They were equal every which way. Nobody was smarter than anybody else. Nobody was better looking than anybody else. Nobody was stronger or quicker than anybody else. All this equality was due to the 211th, 212th, and 213th Amendments to the Constitution, and to the unceasing vigilance of agents of the United States Handicapper General.[3]

In this delightfully ironic yet worrisome tale, Vonnegut portrays a future society in which all differences, all particular and unique human talents and gifts, have been compensated for downward to achieve the "equal society," in the belief that differences in themselves constitute inequalities. Thus ballet dancers, naturally gifted and trained to be lithe and limber, must dance with huge weights and irons on their legs so that they cannot leap any higher or move any more gracefully than anyone else. The world of perfect equality, one in which nobody is better at anything than anybody else, is at last attained! Of course, none of us would care to inhabit Vonnegut's fictional world. That is his point.

In education and the academy, the equation of equality with sameness led to a muddleheaded assault on any notion of distinctiveness or value. A "core curriculum," for example, was jettisoned at many institutions on the presumption that the core was suited only for elitists and hampered individual liberty. Some colleges and universities gave up grading students altogether or adopted a "pass/fail" system, which often amounted to the same thing. Textbook publishers knowingly began to "dumb down" texts in history, science, and literature. In an understandable and justifiable urge to improve the lot of the many, the distinctiveness of the one was forgotten, even disdained.

In his poignant autobiography about growing up as the son of Mexican immigrant parents in California and becoming a "scholarship kid," Richard Rodriguez wrote about the condescending paternalism he encountered all too often at the hands of interventionist egalitarians. His target is affirmative action and his legal categorization as a "minority" as part of educational efforts made in his behalf. Although he received an excellent parochial and public education, he was treated as a victim of cultural deprivation; the working assumption, of course, was that he was both ignorant and incapable of defending himself. All sorts of "allowances" were made for poorly educated Mexican American students and they were pushed through the system under the assumption that standards of merit and achievement were impositions by the Anglo majority on all minorities.

In the name of equality, of promoting "integration" and leveling, political radicals and school administrators often acted in deeply paternalistic ways. As Rodriguez explained:

The conspiracy of kindness became a conspiracy of uncaring. Cruelly, callously, admissions committees agreed to overlook serious academic deficiency. I knew students in college then barely able to read, students unable to grasp the function of a sentence. I knew non-white graduate students who were bewildered by the requirement to compose a term paper and who each day were humiliated when they couldn't compete with other students in seminars. . . . Not surprisingly, among those students with very poor academic preparation, few completed their courses of study. Many dropped out, blaming themselves for their failure. One fall, six nonwhite students I knew suffered severe mental collapse. None of the professors who had welcomed them to graduate school were around when it came time to take them to the infirmary or the airport. And the university officials who so diligently took note of those students in their self-serving totals of entering minority students finally took no note of them when they left.[4]

Unsurprisingly, at the time his book was published, in the early 1980s, there were concerted attempts to discredit Rodriguez as a stalking-horse for right-wing reaction; in this way, his arguments could be ignored, and the general inability of the Left to tolerate diversity in the ranks of minority groups—presumably they should all think alike and have identical needs that can be ministered to—was made evident. This situation has grown even more pronounced since then.

Remember, these assumptions were made with a grim determination to promote sameness in the name of educational and civic equality. Consider how quickly things have changed or, more to the point, how quickly the rhetoric of difference has supplanted the rhetoric of equality—perhaps the better to promote homogenizing ends. I recall my perplexity at a conference on women and feminism in the late 1980s, when I listened to two and a half days of assaults on the very idea of equality. Equality meant "the same." Equality was the mark of masculinism. Equality was the stigma of heterosexism. Equality was pretty much every nasty thing you could come up with and name. Somehow even the Nazis got to be perverse egalitarians in their rush to exterminate the different.

Equality, I learned, meant "homologization with the male subject." As that was news to me, I decided I needed to ponder this matter further. The rush to eliminate equality from our political idiom and our political aspiration struck me as daft. Recognizing that democracy without equality is an impossible proposition, I got the uneasy feeling—one that remains with me and has only been strengthened by recent celebrations of difference as a uniform and fixed group identity—that perhaps many of those who are immersed in what they call the "discourse of difference" are not so keen on constitutional democracy itself. One participant in the conference was candid about this point. Women, she claimed, should be celebrating their "will-to-power." Democratic equality was both "puny and phony." She evidently neither knew nor cared about the ways that slogan had been disastrously deployed in the not-too-distant past. I refer, of course, to the perverse use of this idea by mid-century haters of democracy, especially in fascist rhetoric and theory. We are not so far removed from these events that we can be blithe about deploying certain slogans uncritically. Perhaps one should not be too concerned, however. Perhaps this is primarily an academic exercise, radical playacting by a few indi-

viduals who would be appalled to see the implication of their
own ideas fully worked out.

But there is room for worry. As the political theorist
George Kateb noted: "To want to believe that there is either a
fixed majority interest or a homogeneous group identity is not
compatible with the premises of rights-based individualism."[5]
Although I prefer to speak of democratic "individuality," rather
than "individualism," Kateb's point is well taken. To the extent
that citizens begin to retribalize into ethnic or other "fixed-
identity" groups, democracy falters. Any possibility for human
dialogue, for democratic communication and commonality,
vanishes as so much froth on the polluted sea of phony equality. Difference becomes more and more exclusivist. If you are
black and I am white, by definition I do not and cannot, in
principle, "get it." There is no way that we can negotiate the
space between our given differences. We are just stuck with
them, stuck in what political thinkers used to call "ascriptive
characteristics"—things we cannot change about ourselves.
Mired in the cement of our own identities, we need never deal
with one another. Not really. One of us will win and one of us
will lose the cultural war or the political struggle. That's what
it's all about: power of the most reductive, impositional sort.

The political theorist Sheldon Wolin fears that the most
important democratic category, the citizen, will dissolve in the
acids of this new ideology of difference, an ideology that
despairs of, or huffily rejects, equality. In this respect, Wolin
defines equality as "some broad measure of similarity if only to
support a notion of membership that entails equality of rights,
responsibilities, and treatment."[6] Repudiating the "sameness" of
equality for its homogenizing urge, ideologues of difference

embrace their own version of sameness—an exclusionist sameness along lines of gender, race, ethnicity, and sexual preference. There is no apparent end to this process, as identities get shaved off into more and more minute slivers, for example, lesbian women of color; "Act-Up" militants who favor outing; white, heterosexual men who were abused by their fathers—the possibilities are endless. Ironically, according to Wolin, it has traditionally been the "nondemocratic rulers, the men who justify their rule by appealing to differences— heredity, divinity, merit, knowledge—who reduce populations to a common condition."[7] We now impose a common condition on ourselves in the name of diversity.

If one sees in democratic principles, including the insistence that we are obliged to reach out to one another rather than to entrench in our isolated groups, only a cover for hidden privileges, one stalls out as a citizen. This leads to a terrible impasse, Wolin concludes, one to which "the politics of difference and the ideology of multiculturalism have contributed by rendering suspect the language and possibilities of collectivity, common action, and shared purposes."[8] Yet, those who push such politics must, in practice, appeal to "some culture of commonality" in launching their demands that their differences be respected and their grievances responded to. There is, in fact, a way it can be done that recognizes both the "difference" and the commonality of an aggrieved group.

Let us consider the discourse on equality and difference as it pertains to persons with developmental disabilities. I can track four stages in the story of equality and difference as it pertains to people with such disabilities. First, the "retarded" are construed as being outside the world of equality, having been identified by others as persons who lack the qualities necessary to play a part in the world of equality and inequality, the world of juridical and civic relations, the world of public freedom. Their difference disqualifies them by definition. Some, of course, even put such persons outside the boundaries of humanity—recall that the mentally handicapped and disabled were the first targets of Nazi extermination policies. In the second stage, the retarded, still called and thought of as such, are drawn within the circle of concern by those who do have a civic identity and are part of the world of democratic equality. The disabled become the recipients of concern; their welfare must be seen to. But they are not yet participants in the drama of democratic equality themselves. In a third phase, the retarded, in and through their "normal" representatives, make claims upon the "equal," arguing that they, too, have the qualifications to be part of the discourse. They, too, can vote and hold jobs—or the vast majority can. They, too, can love and be loved. So, over time, they are incorporated on the presumption that they are not so "different" as was once assumed. Finally, the developmentally different find their own voice, however halting, and insist that their difference does not sever them from equality.

In vital ways, persons with disabilities are more like than unlike those without disabilities. But because of the ways they are unlike the majority, they must struggle to make the case for equality with respect for difference. They seek recognition. Language shifts: We are not "retards," they implore us; we are your fellow citizens with disabilities. Equality, or entering the discourse of equality, does not and need not have to do with homogeneity. Instead, equality remains a powerful term of political discourse and an instrument for social change and justice, one of the strongest weapons the relatively powerless have at their disposal to make their case and define their aims before their fellow citizens.

But if you have consigned equality to the discursive trash heap as so much phony-baloney, as we used to say as children, and scream at me that you will have none of it; if, instead, you insist that what politics must consist of is my acknowledging and recognizing your differences but not being allowed to engage you about these differences directly because we have nothing to say to each other, then I can only respond that you are not thinking and acting like a democratic citizen. You are thinking and acting like a royal pain in the neck, and the sooner I can get you out of my sight and mind, I will—not because I am racist or sexist or any of the other handy labels we toss around all too easily these days, but because I am weary of being accused of bad faith no matter what I do, or say, or refrain from doing or saying.

MULTICULTURALISM AND DEMOCRATIC EDUCATION

How did we get into this mess? There are many reasons, including the unraveling of democratic civil society I discussed in chapter 1. Here I want to focus on another dimension of the trials of contemporary democracy: education. American public education is in big trouble and has been since at least the 1970s. Defenders of public schools are on the defensive. Most

often they portray themselves as embattled champions of
democracy against repressive right-wingers, evangelical hotheads, and irrational and unenlightened parents. Now, there
are no doubt repressive types and hotheads and overwrought
parents engaged in skirmishes with educational institutions,
from preschools to universities. But critics do not neatly fit this
demeaning and misleading picture.

Bear in mind that it was taken for granted from the start
of the American democratic experiment that the survival of the
republic for any length of time would depend heavily on the
cultivation of civic sentiments among the young. The optimistic hope was that a national character could be formed by
the careful molding of each generation's children. This hope
had a long and noble lineage. In his great funeral oration, Pericles marked the difference between the Spartan system, which
subjected young boys to harsh and laborious training replete
with grim martial restrictions, and the open Athenian system of
generosity and leniency. Like the Spartans, the Athenians were
brave in battle; unlike the Spartans, they promoted goodwill,
what we today might call "well-roundedness." (I discuss Pericles' funeral oration in more detail in chapter 4.)

The American Founders debated education, rejecting
explicitly a classic civic republican education modeled on the
Spartan example because it demanded and likely yielded
homogeneity and sameness. In *Federalist Number 10,* Publius
advanced a commitment to civility, one that implies acceptance of difference as well as political equality. The "spirit of
the people," informed by religious principles and a belief in
nature and nature's laws, required no prefixed and dogmatic
creed. This epistemological version of difference involved the

awareness of different opinions: We do not all think alike. In contrast, the claims to difference of many contemporary multi-culturalists are couched in ontological terms: This is what we *are*. According to this vision of exclusive groups, there is such a thing as "thinking black" or "thinking white"; you can't help it, if you are one or the other. To the extent that public schools put themselves at the service of this latter version of multicul-turalism, they disastrously abandon the turf they were deeded, the space within which they were enjoined to help create a commitment to a rough-and-ready social egalitarianism, cou-pled with an equally strong commitment to civility.

But how can imposed uniformity—whether of same-ness or of difference—prepare citizens of a democracy to exercise civic and social responsibilities? This is a worry that many now have about the educational wars being waged in America over so-called multicultural curricula that are designed explicitly to entrench differences. The new multi-culturalism promotes, as I noted earlier, incommensurability: If I am white and you are black, we cannot, in principle, speak to or understand each other. You just don't and won't "get it." As a form of ideological teaching, multicultural abso-lutism isolates us in our own skins and equates culture with racial or ethnic identity. Some critics have described this as a process of "resegregation" and wonder how long it will take to move from separate approaches for black children in the name of Afro-centricity, for example, to a quest for separate schools. One of the glories of American public education has been its mingling of class, gender, ethnicity, and race. That was part of the democratic ethos. In *Days of Obligation,* Richard Rodriguez noted:

American educators have lost the confidence of their public institution. . . . There are influential educators today,
and I have met them, who believe that the purpose of
American education is to instill in children a pride in their
ancestral pasts. Such a curtailing of education seems to
me condescending; seems to me the worst sort of mis-
sionary spirit. Did anyone attempt to protect the white
middle-class student of yore from the ironies of history?
Thomas Jefferson—that great democrat—was also a slaveowner. Need we protect black students from complexity?
Thomas Jefferson, that slaveowner, was also a democrat.
American history has become a pageant of exemplary
slaves and black educators. Gay studies, women's studies,
ethnic studies—the new curriculum ensures that education will be flattering. But I submit that America is not a
tale for sentimentalists.[9]

If we are flattered and cajoled into thinking ours is a
story of purity because it is one of victimization, we become
sentimentalists. As Rodriguez went on to insist, newcomers to
this country need to know about seventeenth-century Puri-
tans and about cowboys and Indians; these are constitutive
dramas of American society. Teaching exotic, mythic, and
"foreign" pasts does not prepare one for a culture that is both
"in common" and forever changing. If I can indulge in yet
another reminder, democracy is not simply a set of procedures or a constitution, but an ethos, a spirit, a way of
responding, and a way of conducting oneself. Not being simple, democracy does not afford us a straightforward answer
to the question of what education in, and for, democracy
might be. If, for example, we move too quickly to the notion
of relevance—teach them something practical, so they can

get jobs when they leave school—we may stress watery adaptation above authentic excellence. If we concentrate exclusively on the few, assuming that the many are less vital in the overall scheme of things, the democratic culture necessary to sustain constitutional democracy over the long haul will either wither on the vine or not bear fruit in the first place. If we say that education must be for the many, and we believe the many are not up to much, we abandon excellence for the lowest common denominator: There goes Jefferson's aristocracy of virtue and talent!

A delicate line separates the overpoliticization of education from the awareness that education is never outside a world of which politics—how human beings govern and order a way of life in common—is a necessary feature. Education is always cast as the means whereby some, or all, citizens of a particular society get their bearings and learn to live with and among one another. Education always reflects a society's views of what is excellent, worthy, and necessary. These reflections are not cast in cement like so many foundation stones; rather, they are refracted and reshaped over time as definitions, meanings, and purposes change through democratic contestation. In this sense education is political, but being political is different from being directly and blatantly politicized—being made to serve interests and ends imposed by militant groups, whether in the name of heightened racial awareness, true biblical morality, androgyny, therapeutic self-esteem, or all the other sorts of enthusiasms in which we are currently awash.

Consider the following examples. A class takes up the Declaration of Independence, with its grand pronouncement that "all men are created equal." But when the Declaration of Independence was written, women (and many men) were disenfranchised, and slaves were not counted as full persons. How could this be, the students wonder? What meaning of equality did the Founders embrace? Were any of them uneasy about it? How did they square this shared meaning with what we perceive to be manifest inequalities? What was debated, and what was not? What political and moral exigencies of that historic moment compelled what sorts of compromises? Might things have gone differently? This classroom is an instance of reflective political education in and for a particular democracy—the American version—and its perennial dilemma of the one and the many.

But let me put forth a second and a third example, exaggerated in order to mark the differences between these latter two instances and my first example as clearly as I can. In a second classroom, the teacher declares that the Founders were correct in every respect. To be sure, slavery was an unfortunate blemish, but it was corrected. As a democratic educator at the end of the twentieth century, she must reaffirm her students' devotion to the Founders and the Republic. After all, did they not distill the essence of the wisdom of the ages, good for all times and all places, in their handiwork? They were statesmen, above the fray, not politicians. Here, uncritical adulation triumphs.

The hagiographer's mirror image is offered by my third teacher, who declares that nothing good ever came from the hand of that abstract, all-purpose villain, the "dead, white European male." The words and deeds of such men, including the Founders, were nefarious. Nothing but racists and patriarchalists, those blatant oppressors hid behind fine-sounding words. All they created is tainted and hypocritical. All is fore-closed. All, presumably, has been exposed. Debate ends or is discouraged. To express a different point of view is to betray a false consciousness, venality, or white, patriarchal privilege. Demonology triumphs.

These two examples of teacherly malfeasance I take to be instances of unreflective, dogmatic politicization. Each evades the dilemmas of democratic equality rather than offering us points of critical reflection on that dilemma. This sort of education fails in its particular and important task of preparing us for a world of ambiguity and variety. It equips us only for resentment or malicious naïveté. Let me be clear: I am not indicting education on any level as the sole author of our growing balkanization. But I am suggesting that the schools, whose mission once was to instill some measure of commonality across differences, now suffer under the claim that that effort itself is but another name for "normalization" and cultural imperialism. All those dedicated teachers in all those public schools—the vast majority of them women—who work long hours for low pay and see their work as a vocation, relegated by some contemporary radicals, including militant multiculturalists, to the status of agents of domination, sometimes witting, sometimes not.

There are two off-kilter positions, then. In one, the mesmerized worshiper of authority, who will brook no criticism of the Founders, denies herself the critical freedom that is hers as an educator and that should be imparted to her students. In the other, the agitated negator of all that has gone before preaches freedom from the dismal and spurious past and what she sees as an all-pervasive and menacing tradition that she would cast off, and she insists that her students see it that way, too. But a genuine education in and for democracy would bring matters to the surface; would help us engage in a debate with interlocutors long dead or protagonists who never lived, save on the page; and, through that engagement, would elaborate alternative conceptions through which to apprehend our world and the way that world represents itself.

"Perhaps," wrote the political philosopher Michael Oakeshott,

> we may think of the components of culture as voices, each the expression of a distinct condition and understanding of the world and a distinct idiom of human self-understanding, and of the culture itself as these voices joined, as such voices could only be joined, in a conversation—an endless unrehearsed intellectual adventure in which, in imagination, we enter into a variety of modes of understanding the world and ourselves and are not disconcerted by the differences or dismayed by the inconclusiveness of it all.[10]

This openness to diverse voices helps to keep alive both our distinctiveness and the possibility of commonalities.

I think of my own education, and my democratic dreams, as they were nurtured in the rural Colorado village in which I grew up. The Timnath Public School, District Number 62, incorporated Grades 1 through 12 in a single building. I remember that we memorized the Declaration of Independence and the Gettysburg Address. When my classmates and I were in Grades 7 and 8, in a single classroom under the firm if somewhat eccentric tutelage of Miss McCarthy, the recitation of the Gettysburg Address was quite an event. We would line up in a single row around the classroom. On Miss McCarthy's signal, we would begin to hum the stirring song of the American Civil War, "The Battle Hymn of the Republic," as Miss McCarthy recited the Gettysburg Address with flourish and fervor. She had a way of trailing off each sentence in a trembly, melodramatic whisper that sometimes left us hummers in stitches. But I never forgot the Gettysburg Address and its promise of democratic equality.

My democratic dream was nurtured by a presumption that none of us is stuck inside our own skins; our identities and our ideas are not reducible to our membership in a race, an ethnic group, or a sex. I remember my father telling me that the "Mexican kids" were sometimes smart and nice and sometimes not, just like other kids. (Mexican was the term of respect in that time and place.) I had learned long before Martin Luther King, Jr., made it the central theme of his great "I Have a Dream" speech that I was to judge others not by the color of their skins but by the content of their character and the quality of their deeds. It would never have occurred to me that I should think girlishly or that my friend Raymond Barros was required to think "with his blood."

Our text for the high school English class in that isolated little place was called *Adventures in Reading*. I still have my copy—I bought it from the school because I loved so many of the stories and poems in it. The table of contents list "Good Stories Old and New," with such bracing subsections as "Winning Against the Odds," "Meeting the Unusual," and "Facing Problems." We read "Lyrics from Many Lands" and "American

Songs and Sketches." I looked at this text recently as I thought about democracy and education. By no means was it dominated by a single point of view, that of the dread dead white European male. We read Mary O'Hara, Dorothy Canfield, Margaret Weymouth Jackson, Elsie Singmaster, Selma Lagerlöf, Rosemary Vincent Benét, Kathryn Forbes, Sarojini Naidu, Willa Cather, and Emily Dickinson, among others. We read the great abolitionist Frederick Douglass and the black reformer Booker T. Washington. We read Leo Tolstoy and Pedro de Alarcón. We read translations of Native American warrior songs.

Now this reading was not done under the specific rubric of multiculturalism. It was undertaken on the assumption that life is diverse, filled with many wonders. Through *Adventures in Reading,* we could make the lives and thoughts of others our own in some way. In my imaginings and yearnings, I did not feel constrained because some of the writers I admired most were men. I later chafed against the constraints I encountered outside my imagination, of course, but education is about opening the world up, not imprisoning us in terms of race, gender, or ethnicity. I was taught, as the preface to the textbook said, that: "Reading is your passport to adventure in faraway places. In books the world lies before you, its paths radiating from great cities to distant lands, to scenes forever new, forever changing. . . . Reading knows no barrier, neither time nor space nor bounds of prejudice—it admits us all to the community of human experience." Clearly, I was a lucky child, a lucky *democratic* child, for I learned that, in Oakeshott's words, "Learning is not merely acquiring information . . . , nor is it merely 'improving one's mind'; it is learning to recognize some specific invitations to encounter particular adventures in human self-understanding."[11]

This work of self-understanding cannot be the exclusive purview of the family or of some overweening state or bureaucracy that is pushing either homogeneity or multiculturalism. It is primarily a task of civil society, of which schools are a part. Of course, education in and for a democratic culture is a porous affair, open to the wide world outside the door and beyond the playground. But that does not mean it must become the plaything of purveyors of passing political or pedagogical enthusiasms. The danger in continuing down our present path is that our understanding of education itself is increasingly imperiled because we have done too little to protect education, and the children being educated, from heavy-handed intrusion by those who would have both education and children serve this political master or that ideological purpose, whether in the name of change or in defense of some status quo. Thus, we increasingly give over to education all sorts of tasks it is ill equipped to handle. At the same time, we seem intent on stripping education of what it ought to be about: an invitation to "particular adventures in human self-understanding."

A democratic drama is the playing out of the story of self-limiting freedom. The danger in any ideological definition of education is that it undermines this essential dimension, in much the way Pericles argued that Sparta undermined authentic, self-chosen civic bravery by mandating harsh and severe sacrifice. Because democracy requires freedom as responsibility, any definition or system that sanctions the evasion of responsibility, as I sink my identity totally into that of a group and its "groupthink," imperils democracy. Education is atomized; civic identity is splintered. Whether in the name of change or to forestall change, an ideological system of education is the worst way for human beings to try to order and to ensure their collective democratic affairs. For once a world of personal responsibility with its characteristic virtues and marks of decency (honor, friendship, fidelity, and fairness) is ruptured or emptied, what rushes in to take its place is politics as a "technology of power," in Václav Havel's words. Responsibility, according to Havel—and he is as surefooted a guide as any currently available—flows from the aims of life "in its essence," these aims being plurality and independent self-constitution, as opposed to the conformity, uniformity, and stultifying dogmas of left- and right-wing ideologues who abandon reality and assault life with their rigid, abstract chimeras.

A fusion of freedom and responsibility yields a distinct but definite political conclusion: Democracy is the political form that permits and requires human freedom, not as an act of self-overcoming or pure reason, but in service to others in one's time and place. Democrats are so concerned with the education of children because, through education, children can get acquainted with the world in a way that will help them assume responsibility. To live "within the truth," as Havel called it, is to give voice to a self and a citizen who has embraced responsibility for the here and now: "That means that responsibility is ours, that we must accept it and grasp it here, now, in this place where the Lord has set us down, and that we cannot lie our way out of it by moving somewhere else, whether it be to an Indian ashram or to a parallel *polis*."[12]

Havel believes we are all living in the midst of a general crisis of human consciousness, which manifests itself in the spheres of human freedom, responsibility, and identity. Accepting the risks of free action—an affirmation that education in and for democracy makes possible but does not guarantee—marks one as a person and forms the basis of one's identity. Any mode of thought or program of education that reduces human responsibility narrows the horizon of human possibility. To assume full responsibility is not to lapse into dour moralism or to universalize a giddy and boundless compassion; rather, it is to take up the specific, concrete burdens of one's culture. Recently, for example, Havel denounced the troubles faced by Eastern Europe's Gypsy population as an example of the search in a post-Communist world, for "pseudo-certainties," identity politics being one of the most readily available and virulent forms of such certainty. Assaults against Gypsies, for not being one of "us," offer "a litmus test not of democracy but of civil society. The two are certainly two sides of the same coin. . . . [W]e have created all the basic institutions of democracy—political parties, a parliament, elections. Now much more effort should be focused on building a civil society, to promote a climate that would encourage people to act as citizens in the best sense of the word. . . ."[13] Public education that undermines the possibility of, and responsibility for, this form of citizenship is an exercise in speciousness.

This is tough stuff. But, then, democracy is for the stout of heart who know there are things worth fighting for in a world of paradox, ambiguity, and irony. This democratic way—moderation with courage, open to compromise from a basis of principle—is the rare but occasionally attainable fruit of the democratic imagination and the democratic citizen in action. Democracy is on trial in our time, beleaguered by foes and bedeviled by friends. But there have always been skeptics. Democracy was both tried and condemned by a number of my distinguished forebears in the world of Western political philosophy. Perhaps it is worth making a brief detour into democracy's contentious past in order to take the most accurate measure we can of the current prospects for democracy.

4

Democracy's Contentious Past

STEPPING back for a moment from democracy's contemporary trials will help us to recall what might be called democracy's perpetual trial. Although democracy enjoys a good press as we enter the waning years of the twentieth century, despite the many trials by fire through which old and new democracies are passing, that has not always been the case. The history of Western politics and Western political thought puts on display a variety of powerful arguments both for and against democracy.

While nowadays no one wants to be thought "antidemocratic," including tyrants, oligarchs, and zealots of whatever stripe, this is a relatively recent development. To call oneself a democrat in previous eras was to court suspicion, even disdain. In our enthusiasm for the word *democracy*, we tend not only to downplay antidemocratic developments in our own society but to forget just how hard-fought the struggle over democracy has been, in texts and assemblies, in schools and streets, in the homes of the bereft and the corridors of the powerful alike.

I ask the reader to return with me to the time and place where the issues at stake between democrats and antidemocrats were first joined: ancient Attica. Modern political philosophers and citizens alike look to our Greek forebears as the fathers of democracy; indeed, we are taught that the Athenians "invented" it. By our contemporary reckoning, it was a rather peculiar democracy, of course: the vast majority of the populace of Athens could not vote, deliberate in assembly, or, indeed, fight in a war—the signal responsibility and privilege of the citizen. Slaves, laborers, and women were excluded from its sphere. Nonetheless, the Athenians proclaimed themselves a special breed, called by the name "democrat," because the minority who were citizens had final say on the actions to be taken by the *polis*, the political community.

PERICLES: THE IMPORTANCE OF DEMOCRATIC RHETORIC

The term democracy was known as early as the seventh century B.C. By the second half of the sixth century, arguments for and against democracy had jelled. As the story is usually told, democrats won the fight for the "hearts and minds" of later generations, including early-modern social contract thinkers, constitutionalists, and political reformers seeking ancient lineage for, and classical legitimation of, many of their own ideas. One need look no further than the American *Federalist Papers* to read the assessments of the pros and cons of democracy, ancient and modern, taken up by the Founders of the American republic. The Founders were well aware of the classical democratic heritage. But they also appreciated the fact that an ancient political philosopher had the better argument—or at least the most elegantly elaborated one—and it was anti- rather than prodemocratic, deeded to later generations by the masterful pen of Plato, the Athenian.[1]

But let us take up the prodemocratic story first, especially as it was articulated in the fullness of rhetorical splendor in the funeral speech of Pericles, a leader in Athens's prolonged war against Sparta, the Peloponnesian War, which convulsed Athens, her allies, and her opponents for nearly thirty years in the fifth century B.C. Pericles' speech has come down to us as it was reconstructed by the great historian of that war, Thucydides. Remember, as backdrop, that arguments for and against democracy had long raged. During the sixth and fifth centuries B.C., many Greek city-states had attained rough-and-ready democratic constitutions, founded on the premise of equality or *isonomia*—the condition said to pertain between and among citizens in whom final political authority was lodged and who determined the course of their city's fate by majority vote.

In Athens, this system had been nearly perfected: an Assembly of the people deliberated, with all who were citizens participating. A selected leader who ruled over or governed the Assembly was first among equals. His position was not a permanent leasehold but a temporary obligation and honor. All citizens could speak freely in the Assembly as part of the law-making process. To its proponents, democracy—the rule of the people—was a glory indeed, a shining example of the liberation of the citizen from the toils of everyday life to enjoy the brisk and bracing freedom of the political realm.[2]

Pericles used the occasion of the burial of Athenian war dead to proffer his paean to Athenian democracy. All later democrats embraced this effort as the most splendid example of *epideictic* oratory (speeches made for public occasions imbued with an explicit political content). In ancient democracy words reigned supreme—in particular, those words uttered to and before one's fellow citizens, indeed, to all Athenians, the people, or *demos*, in general, on the solemn occasions of the burial of war dead. Nicole Loraux, a classical scholar, goes so far as to claim that Athenian democracy was "invented" through rhetoric, especially the funeral oration, a practice not only proper to but peculiar to that premier democratic city, Athens. "In and through the funeral oration," she writes, "democracy becomes . . . a name to describe a model city."[3]

Why, then, is Pericles' speech taken as exemplary? Because he uses the solemn ritual of burying the first war dead in the struggle against Sparta to do more, much more, than honor those who "shall not have died in vain," in the words of Abraham Lincoln's Gettysburg Address, very much modeled after the ancient example. Pericles uses his oration to define and to refine Athenian democracy and to explain why sacrifice in her name was a worthy and noble thing. He emphasizes the uniqueness of Athens, not simply its constitution and laws but the qualities of mind and habit that define what it means to belong to that democratic city. Athenians are not, like the Spartans, forced by a "painful discipline" to conform. Rather, they are self-conscious citizens and patriots. The dead have chosen the city over their own lives.

Pericles defines democracy for the gathered assembly, including mothers and fathers there to bury their beloved sons, in these words:

> Our constitution is called a democracy because power is in the hands not of a minority but of the whole people. When it is a question of settling private disputes, everyone is equal before the law; when it is a question of putting one person before another in positions of public responsibility, what counts is not membership of a particular class, but the actual ability which the man possesses.

But there is something other than just the more or less codified, legal provisos of a democratic way of life as laid out in the constitution or *politeia*. Pericles extols the "day-to-day" relations of Athenians with "each other," the practices and spirit of the people. For we "do not get into a state with our next-door-neighbor if he enjoys himself in his own way, nor do we give him the kind of black looks which, though they do no real harm, still do hurt people's feelings. We are free and tolerant in our private lives; but in public affairs we keep the law. This is because it commands our deep respect." It is the "laws themselves" that are obeyed, including the "unwritten laws which it is an acknowledged shame to break." We Athenians, he says, love beauty; we are open to the glory of words and deeds; "our city is an education to Greece"; future ages will honor us. Therefore, he tells the grieving crowd, "fix your eyes every day on the greatness of Athens, as she really is, and . . . fall in love with her." Freedom depends on courage and honor. The dead offer us examples of both.[4]

These are stirring words—the sort of oratory we Americans used to expect on the Independence Day and other civic holidays when they were not so much an opportunity to play golf or go fishing or watch television as a community occasion for reciting and listening to the words of the Declaration of Independence and that unparalleled example of American political oratory, Lincoln's Gettysburg Address, extolling a government "of the people, by the people, and for the people" and praying that it shall never "perish from the earth."

PLATO: THE ARGUMENT AGAINST DEMOCRACY

Plato, it must be said, would have none of this. Even Aristotle, his more moderate successor, while less harsh in his strictures against democracy, nevertheless reckoned it a big gamble and thought a democratic constitution not the one most devoutly to be wished. A reminder is needed here of what democracy entailed—what fueled Plato's ire—before we take the measure of his powerful discontents in this matter. Ancient democracy affirmed the "sovereign power of the demos with a recognition of majority law, based on the equality of the citizens."[5] This equality meant equality in the *agora*, the open place where citizens assembled and debated, where rhetoric took primacy. Government was not by *all* the people, given the restrictions of citizenship, but it must be *for* all the people. For her defenders, like Pericles, democracy was the name given to the model city in which the power of the people and of law, political liberty and freedom of speech, political equality and rotation of offices, and, above all, justice between and among citizens defined political life. Lincoln took his own stab at offering a brief definition in the form of an elegant three sentences. In 1858 he wrote, "As I would not be a *slave*, so I would not be a *master*. This expresses my idea of democracy. Whatever differs from this, to the extent of the difference, is no democracy."[6] Lincoln, the master rhetorician and writer of American democracy, knew a good turn of phrase and coined many himself.

Plato, as I already noted, was not happy with democrats in his own time, and he would no doubt be appalled by ours. Lincoln's democratic sentiments and his search for the nobility of the common man would have driven Plato to despair. Had not a corrupt Athenian democracy put to death that noblest of men, the philosopher Socrates? "With all due respect, Mr. Lincoln," he might write, "your definition of democracy is not nearly so airtight, not the ringing bell echoing through the stillness of a glorious, unending democratic sunrise, stirring the hearts of all who hear the sound, as you appear to believe. Democracy, the American experiment, the 'last best hope on earth'? Count me out," I hear Plato grumble, and I imagine him going on to chide Lincoln for the overly literal definition Lincoln proffers of *slave* and *master*, hence of democracy itself.

"You seem to think," Plato might say to Honest Abe, "that slavery is merely a matter of ownership in another, where one, the slave, is legally and politically unfree and the other, the master, enjoys his freedom, including the freedom to own the slave and to benefit from his unpaid labor, labor that frees the master for nobler pursuits. But the subjection of some is in fact a precondition for the only authentic freedom—not that of the master but of the wise and virtuous person. In my ideal city, I call these paragons Guardians, for they have defeated the worst slavery, their own slavery to baser instincts and passions. The actual indenture of the corrupted many to the wise few is a matter of little consequence by contrast to the wholly legitimate triumph by the few over those baser passions that enslave the many and suit them only to an inferior status."

Lincoln, hearing this, would no doubt tweak Plato a bit, a twinkle in his eye. I hear him intone in that high-pitched Kentucky-Illinois nasal drawl said to characterize his speech: "Why, Mr. Plato, I fear no one has delved deeper into the well of knowledge than you appear to have done and come up dryer. How can one know, save through democratic give and take, the rough and tumble of politics itself, who is wisest and who is best? Who is the slave to passion and who possesses the wisdom to govern?" Let us imagine Mr. Lincoln leaving the room at this point and giving Plato the floor. Lincoln has other things to tend to, perhaps writing the Gettysburg Address to deliver to those who have gathered to honor the dead of the terrible civil war convulsing the American republic.

What is Plato so exercised about? Why, to this day, is he considered the most potent of all antidemocratic philosophers? Why, indeed, is it that among political philosophers, democracy has never enjoyed the unambiguous good press it has long received among ordinary citizens in the West and much of the world, a world now witness to all sorts of dramatic transformations that go by the name "democracy" and march to democracy's tune, understood as self-determination, self-respect, and a recognition of human rights? Well, Plato's fears are many. For him, democracy is dangerous; it represents a derangement of the right order of things. To evaluate Plato's sustained screed against democracy, let us briefly take the measure of ancient deliberation of the systematic or philosophic sort about democracy.

The Greeks reckoned democracy one of the possible political forms or constitutions. Being fond of typologies, they enumerated the characteristics of different constitutions and then rank-ordered them from best to worst. Plato goes along with the typologies of forms of constitutions and, of these forms in their noncorrupt varieties, democracy is ranked lowest. In his masterwork of the political imagination, *The Republic*, Plato stresses the degenerate forms and democracy is degenerate indeed.

Plato's case against democracy, presented in the words of Socrates, is philosophical, epistemological, and political. The political argument is stark and simple: Democracy deteriorates into "license," as people do whatever they want, whenever something much lower in Plato's ranking of human possibilities than "the spirit" moves them. All sorts of unchecked dispositions are given free rein. Rhetoricians, cast by Plato, through Socrates' words, as unscrupulous men who manipulate through speech, take over the souls of the young with their "false and boasting speeches and opinions." True speech is banished, the authentic gold driven out by the tinny dross of what is pleasing and popular.

Listen to the precise terms of Plato's excoriation—the reference point here is the rhetoricians, purveyors of cheap democratic faith of the most corrupt sort:

> once they have emptied and purged [the good] from the soul of the man whom they are seizing ... they proceed to return insolence, anarchy, wastefulness, and shamelessness from exile, in a blaze of light, crowned and

accompanied by a numerous chorus, extolling and flattering them by calling insolence good education; anarchy,
freedom; wastefulness, magnificence; and shamelessness,
courage.[7]

Not a pretty picture. These corrupted democratic speechifiers
and their minions are idle: They neglect everything, they
engage in politics by jumping up and down over transient
enthusiasms, they want to make a lot of money, and they seek
to gratify all desires instantly. In this hellish world, slaves and
men and women become free in identical ways, another sign
of the ultimate in freedom as license and moral turpitude.

That is the political story. But behind it lies a denunciation by Plato of political rhetoric—the echoing resonances of
the spoken word aimed explicitly at democratic ends and of
an epistemology that extols the true knowledge of the tran-
scendent Forms achieved only by the wise and denigrates the
"mere opinion" that is the base lifeblood of the many. Dis-
heartened by the treatment sometimes accorded just men on
this earth, Plato would create a world in which the just are not
only secure from the hounds at their heels but also hold
absolute power. Plato would preclude the debate and contro-
versy of those heated assemblies—these invite only chaos and
discord. The wise, however, know one can attain certitude and
finality only through a complex dialectic that leads to transcen-
dent and unchanging Truth. Plato seeks a few good men—
Philosophers—to rule. These wise few, who have glimpsed
and made their own true knowledge, must serve as physicians
to treat the terrible sickness of society.

Plato sharply divides rhetoric from dialectic, opinion from
knowledge. The high-minded search for Truth looks nothing

like those forensic feats in the Athenian assembly, or even Pericles' funeral oration. Plato's dialectic of knowledge is set up in opposition to a democratic rhetoric of persuasion. He tackles those called Sophists, who plied rhetoric professionally, by calling them mere panderers. In the Platonic dialogue that bears the name of Socrates' hapless interlocutor, the rhetorician Gorgias, Socrates maneuvers Gorgias into declaiming that speech making is not concerned with helping the "sick"—the vast multitude to whom Plato's physician would bring philosophic and political health—learn how to live in order to become well; rather, it involves only freedom for oneself, the power of ruling by convincing others to concur with one's argument. Gorgias is trapped by Socrates into admitting that oratory is not about right or wrong but mere persuasion, a "spurious counterfeit of a branch of the art of government"— the branch known as "democracy."[8]

Democracy in Plato's scheme of things contains no authentic or meaningful speech, only the babble of the ignorant. The ignorant are stuck in mere opinion and give in to base instinct. Hope lies with, as Plato puts it, "the more decent few" who can master desire. From this "smallest group" that comes to share in the only knowledge legitimately called "wisdom," a city may arise "worthy of the philosophic nature."[9] Plato has a cure. He elaborates it in his "ideal city," *The Republic*. Whether he hopes for its actual implementation is, of course, unclear. Most subsequent philosophers think he held forth no such prospect. Some even suggest he was being ironic about the whole business. But later antidemocrats took his arguments to heart, some aspiring themselves to be among the few public-spirited men who ruled for the common good.

A brand-new order, one free from the corrupt democratic taint, is a hard thing to attain: Plato acknowledges this at the outset and throughout his text. The people are so easily misled and aroused. Thus, wise rulers must forbid speeches about the gods and expunge all tall tales of ancient heroes, for poetry inflames the many. The ruler must lie for the benefit of the city. If the ideal city is to come into being, rulers must take "the dispositions of human beings; as though they were a tablet—which, in the first place, they would wipe clean. And that's hardly easy."[10] Though Plato appears to want us to have empathy for his rulers, faced with an arduous task, a more likely response is concern for who or what is to get "wipe[d] clean." As well, the achievement of a just state, a perfect anti-democracy, requires the creation of such a powerful, all-encompassing bond between individuals and the state that all social and political conflict disappears, discord melts away, and the state comes to resemble a "single person," a fused, nearly organic entity.

Away, then, with private marriage, family life, and child rearing, at least for the Guardian class, who must have no competing loyalties other than their wise devotion to, and rule over, the city. A systematic meritocracy must prevail in which children are shunted about like raw material to be turned to the good of the unified city. It works like this: A child from the lower orders of society, those stuck in the mire of ignorance, may perchance show discernible sparks of future wisdom. If so, that child must be removed from his or her parents at once, "without the smallest pity," and trained to be one of the brightest and the best. Plato's explicit purpose with this social engineering is to prevent the emergence of hereditary oligarchies and to ensure the continuation of rule by the best. Thus, a system of eugenics is devised among his Guardians to match up males and females with the most likely mates to produce vigorous, healthy offspring. Immediately after birth, a baby is removed from its biological mother and sent to a central nursery, where its rearing is entrusted to experts. Guardian women who have given birth nurse infants but not their *own*. Each mother nurses the anonymous baby presented to her when she enters the segregated children's quarter of the city. Should a mother get to know her own infant, she would have a private loyalty at odds with her unitary bond to the city; moreover, should the infant be inferior, it would be sent "down" to the lower orders, and a mother bonded to her baby would make a ruckus about such a necessary move. Plato wants no messes in this Guardian encampment.

Well, this system is stern medicine indeed and singularly unattractive to the democratic temperament. Yet it is precisely that temperament Plato denigrates and would eradicate. Why? To what end is all the wrenching he proposes? What does he fear? The only solution Plato sees to individual malaise and social corruption is a world in which individuals get slotted into niches along predetermined and unchanging criteria: Are they up to the task of attaining wisdom, of moving beyond mere opinion, or not? Private homes and sexual attachments, devotion to friends, dedication to individual aims and purposes all militate against single-minded devotion to the ideal city or a quest for Truth.

We see in Plato's strictures that disparagement of rhetoric goes hand in hand with disdain for the vulgar unseemliness of democratic politics. It is a thorn in his side that the wisest and best may not rule over those less wise and less noble. But we also see displayed what might be called the prototypical anti-democratic fear: that things will easily fall apart if a city is divided. Scattered throughout *The Republic* are words that evoke a sense of chaos and disintegration: asunder . . . destroy . . . dissolves . . . overwhelms . . . splits . . . evil. And other terms are designated as potent enough to prevent the anarchy that democracy leads to: dominate . . . censor . . . expunge . . . conform . . . bind . . . make one. For Plato, every conflict is a potential cataclysm; every discussion in which differences are stated a threat portending disintegration; every sally an embryonic struggle unto death; every distinction a possible blemish on the canvas of harmonious and unsullied order.[11]

Fear of disorder is a major hand, even a trump card, for antidemocrats historically. Taking a cue from Plato, later thinkers, devoted to the idea that there must be one overarching truth in a political system, one final voice, one unifying will, fretted excitedly about the anarchy they saw lurking, even smirking menacingly, in the dark shadows of sunny democratic vistas. The democratic commitment to political freedom stirs up ceaseless disputation, they cry. The democratic devotion to *isonomia*, the principle of equality, riles the man or woman who looks with envy on his or her neighbor and wants "the same," for that is how equality is understood by ordinary folk, they warn. History teaches us that popular rages of all kinds flow from this construction, or misconstruction, of what democratic equality requires or demands.

ARISTOTLE: THE GOOD CONSTITUTION
AND THE GOOD LIFE

A more moderate way of working this problem out was proposed by Aristotle, a philosopher far more friendly to democracy than Plato, though still wary. Aristotle distinguishes between good and bad constitutions: Each good constitution can degenerate into a bad form. Democracy, Aristotle claims, is the corrupt form of popular government. It is corrupt because within it the mass of people, the poor, take over and do so in a way likely to lead to violence and anarchy as laws are abandoned and unchecked self-interest triumphs. A good constitution, for Aristotle, is directed to the common interest—whether it is a monarchy or a *politeia*, a constitution of and for the people. But a bad or perverted constitution is captured by selfish interests, whether of a few or the majority. For Aristotle, this is baneful because the end of the state is not "mere life" but a "good life," and a good life is one of felicity and fairness.[12]

Aristotle feared democracy as a form of mobocracy, but he also rejected his revered predecessor's solution to that fear because he claimed that Plato's cure would be worse than the disease: His ideal city would produce a bad form of unity, lead to one-man rule, and ignore justice. For this reason, Aristotle is often turned to as an antidote to Plato's stringently antidemocratic creed, despite Aristotle's own misgivings about democracy.

HOBBES: "ALL AGAINST ALL"

At this point, I want to take up the worries and words of one more antidemocrat who numbers among the handful of universally acknowledged great political philosophers in the Western tradition: Thomas Hobbes. From his seventeenth-century vantage point, Hobbes held that a society could be run on a single principle: recognition that human beings are isolated monads driven by appetite and aversion. Hobbes's central concern was order. The manner in which he conceived alternatives—either anarchy or absolutism—precluded any consideration of other possibilities and, as we have already noticed with Plato, is characteristic of those who fear democracy. The threat of destruction is the basis of the Hobbesian solution to the problem of order on all levels and in each arena of human intercourse. Even the hapless child in the family agrees to be ruled absolutely—in effect, signs a coercive contract—from fear of death at the hands of the parents. All human beings, for Hobbes, are anxious, fearful, threatening to themselves and others, full of inherent destructive passions. Hobbes views life before the creation of commonwealths as a terrifying and conflict-ridden state of nature, a "war of all against all," in his famous, or infamous, words.

To protect ourselves from our neighbors or a restless marauder, we make a deal: We agree to be ruled absolutely by a sovereign, Leviathan by name. He is an all-powerful earthly lord who enjoys the strength conferred on him by all others and reduces all particular wills "unto one Will" in order that there might be, in Hobbes's inimitable language, a "reall Unitie of them all, in one and the same Person. . . . This is the Generation of that Mortall God, to which wee owe under the Immortall God, our peace and defense." This mortal God may judge all opinions, name all names, defend all things as "necessary to Peace, thereby to prevent Discord and Civill Warre."[13] There is a terrible equality in Hobbes's world, but it is not the democratic ideal; rather, it is the equality of the fearful, the equality of human beings so similar in power that any one may kill any other. The less strong can make up for his lack of brawn by grabbing a bludgeon and bashing his neighbor's brains out as he sleeps.

To all who find this a distressing, even repellent, view of the human condition and its prospects, Hobbes suggests that we take a look around. Consider how much we fear. Muse on what price we would pay were we caught up in a world of hideous dislocations, sudden and violent death, and rampaging ne'er-do-wells. Throughout history, there have been those who have sought or imposed Hobbesian solutions. In his own way, Hobbes was a utopian—one who believed that a dramatic move to create an all-powerful sovereign could rescue humanity from its travail. His solution was by no means democratic, but at least one could sleep at night. Peace comes at a heavy price.

ANTIDEMOCRATS IN MODERN TIMES

But not all antidemocrats are disdainful of democracy, as was Plato, or scared out of their wits by it, as was Hobbes. There

are others—syndicalists, romantic utopians, revolutionary
socialists, some existentialists—for whom democracy is to be
repudiated because it is pitiful, an exercise in bourgeois banal-
ity in which the bland lead the bland down the narrow path-
way of cultural conformism and self-interest wrongly understood, as all self-interest, in the long run, is bound to be.
Democracy is for the faint of heart, the effeminate. (Gendered
terms of derision are used here knowingly, for one continuing
gripe about democracy is that it negates the possibility for
heroic action of the manly sort. The man—in Latin, *vir*—gets
few opportunities to put on public display his *virtù*—his ability
to get things done with aplomb and heroic savoir faire.)

Machiavelli muttered dark and cunning things in this
vein, being in the mold of energetic civic republicans who
cherished the autonomy of the city but held out little hope for
a democratic constitution of the sort we moderns would recognize. Rousseau, following suit, held up antidemocratic Sparta
with its martial valor as his great ancient exemplar, not democratic Athens with its public speech and equality among those
eligible for citizenship. Although Rousseau is often numbered
among the great democratic thinkers, his martial enthusiasms
and insistence that the polity be as one, that the national will
not be divided, and that the citizen take on an altogether new
identity as his very will and person become part of "the common" suggest a monistic drive ill suited to the democratic temperament. Remember Pericles' funeral admonition: Democracy
is about more than the constitution and laws; it is about the
habits and dispositions and everyday doings of a people.

That the everyday doings of ordinary people should be
taken into account, even accorded some political weight and

respect, drives utopians around the bend. Twentieth-century revolutionaries, many of them Marxist in their orientation and faith, turned ugly indeed in their attempt to create a unitary order, a utopia cured of capitalist perfidy and democratic hypocrisy. Pity the poor bourgeois householder, they moaned. He will disappear, and in his place will be the militant, the revolutionary, with his enemies to expose, his foes to fight, his world in which whole peoples must triumph or vanish.

If your aim is a unitary order, a perfect regime in which all good things coexist in perpetuity, the give-and-take of democracy is thin gruel indeed. Lenin and such fascist ideologues as Mussolini held democracy in contempt. Lenin celebrated the coming of World War I as a way to cleanse the world of the pathetic, petit bourgeois. So did many on the other side of the political spectrum: A great European war promised purging and redemption to antidemocratic intellectuals and activists on the Left and the Right. For example, a group called the Futurists, aesthetes devoted to purification through violence, shared Lenin's contempt for the world of constitutional democracy and his conviction that its destruction must be ruthless and total if reconstruction was to be permanent. War, they proclaimed, would wipe out "moralism, feminism, every opportunistic or utilitarian cowardice."[14] Democracy, of course, is the political expression of that despised cowardice in fulminations of this sort, past and present.

We hear similar proclamations today. I have already noted the disdain for democratic moderation and coalition building on the part of some contemporary celebrants of multiculturalism and group difference. Those loudly and violently promoting the virtues of ethnic nationhood hate democracy and the promise of civil society. What we see unfolding in the Balkans is a very old phenomenon, one from which our own society is by no means exempt. Going beyond rightful claims to self-respect and civic equality, ethno-cultural absolutists insist that identities must not be mixed. This is a view that civic pluralists, who embrace and affirm the idea that we can and must reach out to others in gestures of solidarity and friendship, cannot accept. As G. M. Tamás puts it, the "ethno-cultural" version of identity and nationalism is that "others ought to be elsewhere; there is no universalistic, overriding, trans-contextual principle 'legitimising' mixture, assimilation or diversity within the same politico-symbolic 'space.'"[15] Those who break political bodies into "warring ethno-cultural enclaves" disdain civic republican and liberal ideas of citizenship, for these accept the possibility of, and, in some instances, the necessity for, a form of national identity not reducible to ethnicity or culture as that which is simply given, flowing ineluctably, as it must, from a prepolitical identity. The "new" ethno-cultural nationalism, "particularly in the extreme shape it has taken in Eastern Europe, cannot and does not want to answer political questions. It is mostly a repetitive reaffirmation of identity." The only precept proffered by the ethno-culturalist as an essentialist prescription is "be what you are."[16] The alternative *civic* ideal is one chastened by the recognition that "others are before and among me," that I am not hunkered down only with others exactly like myself.

In light of democracy's current trials, domestic and foreign, it is important to remember the reason for Solidarity in Poland, Civic Forum in Czechoslovakia, and the independence movements in the Baltic States and other Eastern European countries: to protest their control by the Soviet Empire, first, because it violates principles of self-determination embedded in international law and shared understandings and, second, because it tramples on basic human rights, including the right to participate in, and help to choose, a way of life. Such appeals are at once universal and particular, tapping old identities but energizing new political recognitions. Peoples who proclaim their devotion to human rights as a universal principle can be held accountable, one hopes, in ways that rapacious, nationalistic destroyers, who scoff at such niceties, cannot. (Though one must, of course, *attempt* to hold them accountable.) This middle way—as an alternative to warring racial and ethnic groupings or the homogenized stability of efficiently managed imperialism—seems to me the only possible course that respects claims to self-determination yet holds forth the prospect of a painfully attained and perhaps, for that reason, even more deeply cherished civic order based on universal principles of recognition.

Religious fundamentalists who insist that politics must be theocratic or Theodosian—equating a particular political order with God's will or design—often find democracy the work of the devil. Perhaps, in response to these charges, a concrete example of the delicate balancing act I endorse is necessary. I rely on reports of Pope John Paul II's visit to the Baltic States in September 1993 for this story. The situation in Lithuania was particularly delicate for John Paul because "Polish nationalists for their part have tried to exploit the alleged mistreatment of the 300,000 strong Polish minority in Lithuania." Thus, being not only pope but also a Pole associated with Polish aspirations to self-determination, John Paul "had to be very careful not to offend Lithuanian sensibilities."

Much of current Lithuania, remember, was once part of Poland. The Lithuanian capital, Vilnius, is Poland's "Wilno," dear to the hearts of Poles everywhere, in part because it is the home of Adam Mickiewicz, the greatest Polish poet. But John Paul, while acknowledging the love Poles have for that particular place, used the Lithuanian name Vilnius throughout his pastoral visit, including the one time he spoke Polish—when he delivered mass in the Polish-language church in that city. For the rest of his visit, "the Pope spoke . . . Lithuanian which he had learnt for the occasion" and this "made a tremendously positive impression on the Lithuanians." The Poles "were not so pleased, but coming from the Pope they had to accept it. The Pope exhorted the Poles to identify fully with Lithuania, and not to dwell on the past—by which he meant not to endlessly recall the time when Vilnius was part of Poland."[17]

This account shows how ethical space can be created or expanded for a form of civic identification sans irredentist or chauvinistic aspirations. One might say that "eternal vigilance is the price of civic moderation." Ideologues who enjoin a world "beyond compromise" scorn democracy as anemic. They, too, want the world to conform to their totalist dreams.

DEMOCRACY, YES; UTOPIA, NO

The quest for a unitary order, a utopia, has been cast from Plato to the present as an argument against democracy, even if what the utopian claims to seek is a more complete, full, or authentic democracy. As Isaiah Berlin reminds us:

> Utopias ... are static. Nothing in them alters, for they
> have reached perfection: there is no need for novelty or
> change; no one can wish to alter a condition in which all
> natural human wishes are fulfilled. The assumption on
> which this is based is that men have a certain fixed, unal-
> tering nature, certain universal, common, immutable
> goals. Once these goals are realized, human nature is
> wholly fulfilled. The very idea of universal fulfillment pre-
> supposes that human beings as such seek the same
> essential goals, identical for all, at all times, everywhere.
> For unless this is so, Utopia cannot be Utopia, for then
> the perfect society will not perfectly satisfy everyone.[18]

The utopian tells us that once the struggle is over all will
be well; problems either will have vanished in the blissful harmony of a perfect order or will somehow be solved without
decisive conflict, with those dissatisfied at the outcome walk-
ing away. Democrats know better: Democracy is precisely an
institutional, cultural, habitual way of acknowledging the per-
vasiveness of conflict and the fact that our loyalties are not
one; our wills are not single; our opinions are not uniform; our
ideals are not cut from the same cloth.

Despite all this, despite the blood shed on the altar of
various ahistoric abstractions—and utopias are always abstract
pictures of a shimmering future not yet reachable because enemies stand in the way of their realization—the antidemocratic
impulse dies hard. A harmony of purposes, ends, virtues, and
identities is achievable *only* if we so thoroughly erode the
bases of human habits, dispositions, and possibilities as we
know and have known them that we willingly engage in radical social surgery. Democrats do not favor wholesale overturn-
ings, in part because the democratic disposition is exquisitely

poised between tradition and change, contestation and conti-
nuity. The utopian thinker finds democratic fears misplaced,
bourgeois temerity, perhaps. Rather, those whose intentions
are benign and hearts are pure will surely succeed, one bright
day, when others have failed.

Oddly enough, then, it is often antidemocrats who find
democracy dull. But for the democrat who is prepared to
embrace the give-and-take of democratic political and civic
life, it is the utopian who threatens the tedium of everlasting
sameness. The antidemocrat approaches the overgrown democratic garden—with its profusion of plants, its weeds and
hybrids mixed together, its tendency to stray out of fixed rows
and its explosion of colors and aromas, bloomings and wilt-
ings—with an oversize can of weed killer. The democrat takes
pleasure in the proliferation. Oh yes, she weeds and prunes
but she does not uproot and she refuses to resort to poison.
Who knows what might get harmed along with the noxious
weeds if she were to threaten the whole garden with such a
cure? In this garden both the humblest daisy and the grandest
lily all find their place.

Take something as commonplace as the vote. For the antidemocrat, the vote is either dangerous because the mob can
outvote the wise, or meaningless because it is a liberal decep-
tion, an "opium of the people." Indeed, even democrats are not
united in their defense of the vote. Many contemporary citizens
disdain the vote or hold out little hope for it. They don't think
their vote means much. But suppose a government decided to
disenfranchise the citizens of a single state or province as an
experiment to see whether the vote was held in as low regard
as antidemocrats insist and some democrats bemoan.

It does not take much of a stretch of the political imagination to conjure up the explosion: the cries against the violation of a basic right and of a constitution guarantee, the denial of democratic equality, and the creation of a class of subjects with no voice. At that point we would all be reminded of just how vital the vote is to any compelling and coherent notion of the *citizen*. In American history, black slaves yearned for the vote as a sign of freedom, women struggled for it as a form of political recognition that would make them, too, part of the democratic drama. To be denied the vote is to be denied equal political standing. It is that simple and that important. Writes George Kateb, a political theorist: "Formal membership in constitutional democracy together with the routine workings of the system tends to raise people out of inferior conditions and the internalized sense of inferiority. The coming of constitutional democracy is a liberation, a liberation of mentality and feelings."[19]

But the vote and other markers of democratic citizenship have fallen on hard times. They have been criticized as too much of a bad thing: votes do not matter; power does, and the vote only cajoles us into thinking we have power—or too little of a good thing: Votes may matter but not much. Having taken the measure of current democratic discontents and ancient antidemocratic arguments, I take up democracy's enduring promise in the final chapter.

5

Democracy's Enduring Promise

"LET freedom ring!"—the cry of democrats throughout the centuries—now echoes 'round the world. What do aggrieved peoples want? Freedom. When do they want it? Now. That, at least, is the story of the recent past. From Tiananmen Square to Wenceslas Square, the rhetoric of protesters, dissidents, and new citizens has been cast in the idiom of freedom. But democratic freedom is a particular sort of freedom, tempered by centuries of hard wisdom that stretch from ancient Attica to the modern Western metropolis. It is decocted civic lore that tells us that human beings are not only capable of great deeds of courage and selflessness but are tempted by power, corrupted by greed, seduced by violence, and weakened by cowardice. It is easy enough to understand why Plato believed, and Aristotle suspected, that human beings were ill suited to democracy: We seem altogether too well suited to licentiousness and anarchy and unscrupulous power seeking.

Recall, briefly, the generous bounty of troubles I bagged in previous chapters: the growth of cynicism and the atrophy

of civil society; too much acquisitive individualism that trans-
lates "wants" into "rights"; an increase in disrespect of, even
contempt for, the rule-governed practices that make democracy work; a politics of displacement that disdains any distinction between public and private and aims to open up all
aspects of life to the harsh glare of publicity; the neglect of
practical politics in favor of proclamations of one's unassail-
able and exclusive identity as a member of a group defined by
race, ethnicity, gender, or sexual preference; and a waning of
our ability to transmit democratic dispositions and dreams to
succeeding generations through education. This is not a pretty
picture. It would seem that our prospects are bleak.

HANNAH ARENDT: THE "GRANDIOSE LUDICROUSNESS" OF REVOLUTION

Have we, then, lost the *res publica*? Is the drama of democracy
in its final act on the stage of the West? Will democratic
prospects elsewhere collapse under the weight of nationalism
or religious fundamentalism? My answer is a cautious no.
Democracy may be in peril, but it remains vibrant and
resilient, the great source of political hope in our troubled
world. Hope, as the political philosopher Hannah Arendt
insisted, is the human capacity that sustains political *being*.
Should hopelessness triumph, then and only then will it be
rightly said that democracy is forlorn. But hopelessness has not
yet triumphed. The practical realm of democratic civil society
and the daily habits that this realm sustains and embodies may

have grown brittle and a bit withered from disuse, but hope remains.

The fact that democracy in its particular constitutional and representative form is now the dream dreamed by democrats everywhere is, in and of itself, remarkable. For it was not always so. In her 1963 book contrasting the French and American revolutions, *On Revolution,* Arendt lamented the fact that young political activists of that era were turning to the French, rather than the American, Revolution for inspiration. Marxists, for example, had little use for America's determined yet cautious democrats, with their constitutional wrangling and their detailed Bill of Rights. The French Revolution ended in disaster, bloodshed, one-man rule, and aggressive nationalism. The American Revolution ended in a remarkably steady world of politics without end. In the next century, that politics would be resilient enough to withstand the bloodiest civil war the world had known up to that time, a war brought about, in large measure, by the Founders' sin of slavery. But to the reckless and the romantic, the American Revolution lacked color and panache, including the grandiosity of vast lurchings and wrenchings of the sort the French Revolution displayed in full.

Before Arendt penned her elaborate defense of the American revolutionary tradition against the "imposed compulsion of ideological thinking" of so much twentieth-century political thought, Albert Camus had warned about Marxist celebrations of the French Revolution as a class war and a glorious example of justifiable revolutionary violence, which were much in vogue in post–World War II Europe. He cautioned against the mystique of the proletariat and the attempt by Saint-Just, Robespierre, and their twentieth-century counterparts Marx and Lenin to fit the world into a theoretical frame that deified a notion of the undivided "will of the people" as a substitute for God himself. Camus excoriated a passion for unity that saw any opposition as treason.[1]

For his efforts, Camus was virtually excommunicated from French intellectual life by Sartre and his comrades in *Les Temps Modernes*. As Sartre and others busied themselves for years with explaining away Soviet terror and supported reinforcing the power of the state if it was a "people's state," Camus stressed *le dialogue* as the form that human sociability takes when it appears as politics. Camus was no naïf. He knew what it meant to fight fascism. He also feared what fighting fascism unleashed, namely, counterterror in the name of an abstract Communist utopia. Revolutionary politics of this totalist stripe destroys sociability, making it impossible to say, "I rebel, therefore we exist"—which sounds pretty wimpy if what you want is to storm the barricades, terrorize the bourgeoisie, and not only take over the state but expand its power enormously.

Camus renounced the claims of politics to aspire to the absolute, believing that democratic politics must chasten this aspiration, not capitulate to it, since a politics without limits destroys democracy. Arendt took a similar path when she distinguished the rights of freedom and citizenship from the generic, unlimited "rights of man" proclaimed by the French revolutionaries. Unlike Saint-Just and Robespierre, the American Founders were realists, aware that human beings will always fall short of an absolute ideal. It follows, according to Arendt, that "the only reasonable hope for salvation from evil and wickedness at which men might arrive even in this world and even by themselves, without any divine assistance," must be the imperfect workings of government, the flawed actions of citizens among citizens.[2] Mindful of human limits, the American revolutionaries shored up the means to check the urge to gain unlimited power. Their new government did not promise a perfect world once all enemies were removed, traitors silenced, and the pure goodness of the people's will articulated; rather, the American democracy held out for a partial redemption only: political hope in contrast to earthly salvation.

Dependent on selectively assimilated memories from antiquity, the French *hommes de lettres* who helped foment the Revolution pursued extreme theoretical abstractions to terrible concrete conclusions. Their "conscious thoughts and words stubbornly returned, again and again, to Roman language, drawn upon to justify revolutionary dictatorship." Oddly, Arendt noted, the various metaphors "in which the revolution is seen not as the work of men but as an irresistible process, the metaphors of stream and torrent and current, were still coined by the actors themselves, who, however drunk they might have become with the wine of freedom in the abstract, clearly no longer believed that they were free agents." Prisoners of history, the makers of the French Revolution plunged headlong into an orgy of repetitive destruction.

In the twentieth century, when the objective conditions were supposedly ripe for the Bolshevik revolution, Lenin and his comrades drew upon a rhetoric and a historic teleology forged from lessons they claimed they had learned from the French Revolution. The trouble, according to Arendt, was that "those who went into the school of revolution learned and knew beforehand the course a revolution must take." It must defeat open opponents. Then it must ferret out and destroy hidden enemies. To do the latter, it must centralize power; expand and strengthen the police; create a layer of spies and functionaries; liquidate hypocrites; and finally, forfeit some of its own. This is a "grandiose ludicrousness," Arendt averred, for its automatic adherence to the claims of revolutionary necessity is compulsive and robotic, unlike the uncoerced actions and reactions of free citizens doing the work of politics.

Arendt also taxed the French revolutionaries for the way they promised to solve the social problems of poverty and misery. The revolutionaries, she explained, believed that because the people are abject and silent by definition, they required spokesmen and champions. But having construed the problems the Revolution was meant to solve in almost eschatological terms, the revolutionaries set in motion a dynamic that restlessly sought targets for correction, reproof, or extinction.

Absolute ends require means without limit. Revolutionary pity is boundless in its bathetic force as long as the suffering are a faceless mass. Distinguishing this abstract pity from genuine compassion, Arendt wrote: "Compassion, to be stricken with the suffering of someone else as though it were contagious, and pity, to be sorry without being touched in the flesh, are not only not the same, they may not even be related." One feels compassion, or comprehends it, only in and through the particular. The moment one generalizes, there is a danger that specificity will be lost and boundless pity will come into play.

Pity *for* is not the same as solidarity *with*. Those who pity without limit develop a thirst for power and gain "a vested interest in the existence of the weak." Abstract pity invites